Teach me to write ...
Non-fiction

A GUIDE FOR TEACHERS

Alan Gibbons

Nash Pollock Publishing

Acknowledgements

The author and publishers would like to thank the following for permission to reprint copyright material: Gareth Owen and Rogers, Coleridge & White Ltd for 'Den to Let' by Gareth Owen, from *Collected Poems for Children* published by Macmillan Children's Books; Gervase Phinn and MBA Literary Agents Ltd for 'School Creatures' by Gervase Phinn, from *It Takes One to Know One*, published by Puffin.

© Alan Gibbons

First published 2005
Published by
Nash Pollock Publishing
32 Warwick Street
Oxford OX4 1SX

10 9 8 7 6 5 4 3 2 1

Orders to:
York Publishing Services
64 Hallfield Road
Layerthorpe
York YO31 7ZQ

The author's moral right is asserted.

ISBN: 1 898255 47 4

Design and typesetting by Black Dog Design, Buckingham
Printed in Great Britain by Hobbs the Printers

Contents

Chapter 1

Non-fiction in the classroom

There is nothing more important in education than the ability to express yourself, both orally and in a written form. It is at the root of academic and professional success. It is also the key to being a successful citizen in today's fast-paced and infinitely complex world. The processing of information, its packaging, presentation and delivery are at the heart of the communication revolution that has affected all our lives.

The first two volumes of this series, dealing with fiction and with poetry, were about writing creatively. Almost all teachers would accept that this entails some level of individuality, that the personality of the child will shine through in the final product. In creative writing even the quirky and downright provocative are generally accepted and hopefully encouraged.

So what goes wrong when we ask children to write non-fiction? I have seen a lot of non-fiction lessons in my near twenty-year teaching career and many have been – well, how shall I put this – as dull as ditchwater and equally unappetising. There was the stunningly mediocre Year 3 lesson about 'How we walk to the classroom door.' There was the ploddingly uninspiring Year 5 lesson about 'How to wire an electric plug.' I did ask if the children were actually allowed to wire the plug. 'Of course not,' I was told. 'Health and Safety.'

Non-fiction lessons have, over the years, tended to be almost entirely teacher-directed. Form is often prioritised over content. In recent years many teachers will have seen veritable tidal waves of bullet points sweeping across their pupils' exercise books, some but by no means all used correctly. They can even turn up in the children's fiction where, let's face it, they just shouldn't be. The success, or lack of it, of a non-fiction lesson comes down to this: are the children being asked to express themselves or are they being asked to express somebody else's priorities?

It is my firm belief that education is child-centred. It is a term which has, from time to time, come in for a lot of criticism, if not downright abuse. But what else is education going to be: teacher-centred, government-centred, target-centred? A genuine focus on the child means that lessons have to appeal to his or her experience, and connect with it. The best lessons feature several key elements: knowledge of the subject, pace, humour, anecdotal illustration, and variety in the kind of work the children are expected to undertake. To be a successful participant in a communication-hungry world, the child has to have a flexible grasp of the skills, conventions and rules of non-fiction writing. By their mid-teens, they should have developed a flexible repertoire of forms and strategies. Many begin to develop this instinctively, of course. Take texting. This is often inventive and humorous. Contrary to the prejudices of some tabloid newspapers, just because youngsters take liberties with spelling conventions doesn't mean they can't spell. Then there is the confidence young people show using computers. I well remember coming away from a particularly uninformative school training session on Information Technology. I failed dismally to catch on. So what did I do? I went home and asked my fourteen year old son to show me!

An English curriculum that is reduced to a diet of comprehensions, précis and copies of teacher-demonstrated templates simply dies of boredom. It also encourages passivity. Children become reliant on the teacher. Ultimately, you can end up with an educational culture in which children need to be spoon-fed answers in order to function at all. Surely, such an environment of dependence runs counter to calls for a multi-skilled, flexible and independent workforce. It doesn't do much to nurture critical, questioning members of a mature democracy either! Teaching non-fiction well requires just as much preparation, just as much stimulus, just as much creativity, as teaching fiction or poetry. So let's look back at what makes a lesson devoted to fiction or poetry successful. This overview should inform our approach to teaching non-fiction too.

To start with, the subject of the lesson has to be something about which the children want to write. Children have to be the *subject*, not the object of the writing process. That means knowing the children's interests. This is certainly not a matter of pandering to the lowest common denominator. Who would want a diet of work about the latest dismal slasher movie or 'reality' TV show, the diet of a disturbingly large minority of children? But ghost stories, fantasy stories, adventure and mystery stories are very popular. Poems about personal experience, popular culture, hopes, dreams and aspirations can grab the attention of most youngsters. Choosing subjects that can interest and engross is one of the classroom teacher's key skills. The area of non-fiction writing is not immune from this concern.

Then, once the subject has been chosen, the teacher needs to know how to combine the rigorous teaching of the main features of the particular genre being taught with a learning environment that stimulates self-expression. Grammar, syntax and structure can be taught in context. Indeed, recent educational research suggests that children learn the tools of self-expression better in the context of an enjoyable creative writing lesson than in one devoted to the distinct teaching of grammar, what some people curiously call 'The Basics', as if meaning is not the most basic of basics. Non-fiction, just because it doesn't immediately strike you as 'creative' or 'imaginative', doesn't have to be dull, and each piece of non-fiction writing doesn't have to be identical.

Take advertising. There are many ways to publicise a hamburger.

You could say this:

Buy a Hammy Hamburger. It weighs a quarter of a pound. It is mostly made of meat. It comes in a bread roll sprinkled with sesame seeds. It tastes quite nice really.

Or this:

Taste a Hammy Hamburger and you'll never let another burger pass your lips. Weighing in at a slobber-licious quarter pound, the Hammy is one succulent sesame bun's worth of meaty flavour.

This is the kind of exaggerated prose which has added countless inches to a generation's waistline. The point is: non-fiction lessons can be just as much fun as fiction or poetry.

So what is the approach I am recommending? To write fiction well, the writer has to employ a number of elements: structure, pacing, characterisation, plotting, tension, description, metaphor, simile, dialogue, internal monologue, shorter/longer sentences, paragraphing, good beginnings/endings.

A good writer doesn't think: 'Ooh, I'm short on figurative language here.' Of course not: as part of the experience of writing, he or she employs all these elements in a complex synthesis. Similarly, the poet can draw on many different elements: line length, structures (e.g. odes, haiku, limericks, clerihews), repeated lines, choruses, metaphor, simile, rhyme, alliteration, beat, rhythm, assonance.

Neither of these lists is in any way exhaustive, but the point should be obvious. A successful fiction or poetry lesson has to achieve a balance. It has to introduce children to some of the tools they can employ to express themselves in the form, but it has to do this in the context of the child's self-expression. Err too far in the direction of prescriptive teaching and the resulting children's work will be uniform, uninteresting and lacking that spark of individuality that characterises any good writing. The pupils also become almost entirely dependent on teacher input. Quite soon, they can expect to be spoonfed and fail completely once they are expected to work independently. Err too far in the opposite direction of 'pure' creativity and the children's work will be utterly formless. Allowing the children to 'just create' without any intervention is negligence. They become frustrated because they are not being equipped with the skills to express themselves effectively. Ultimately, there is no progression. Teaching writing involves balancing direction and creativity, prescription and self-expression. Grammar should not be ignored but situated in an engaging context. This tension is what has made the teaching of writing such a controversial area of the curriculum.

What, then, does the teacher of non-fiction need to do? Teaching fiction, you need to demonstrate the features of a successful story while giving children the space to go in whatever direction they wish. Teaching poetry, you need to offer different structures and templates within which they can develop their own ideas. Teaching non-fiction, you do something similar. Non-fiction, as indicated above, works by using a series of conventions and rules to put across information. By identifying these conventions, then using them to structure the piece of non-fiction writing, you are helping your pupils achieve successful self-expression.

A varied, imaginative and stimulating series of lessons can systematically introduce pupils to the forms, conventions and rules of non-fiction. As the children mature and progress they are introduced to more testing skills. The youngsters can then develop an understanding of the many ways in which non-fiction works without having to endure a diet of didactic and unexciting teaching. It is all about achieving that all-important balance between learning new skills and developing independent self-expression.

The rules and conventions

The lessons in this book will cover a range of non-fiction forms:
- instructions
- recipes
- guides and brochures
- reports
- interviews
- advertisements
- biographies
- autobiographies
- debates
- arguments/speeches/presentations
- posters
- letters
- invitations

Each of these forms has a set of identifiable conventions and rules. Let's take a couple of examples. When you are writing a letter, you put the address and date in the top right-hand corner. The phrase *Dear ...* with which you address your reader goes over on the left hand side. Then there is the text and finally, *Yours faithfully* or *Yours sincerely*. Alternatively, depending on the nature of the letter, you could use *With best wishes* or *Yours* or just *Love*.

Again, when you are writing a piece of persuasive writing, there are certain phrases you tend to use. It is common to address the reader directly: *Let's consider ...* You might employ questions: *Do you really think that ...? Could anybody really believe ...?* There will be connectives. These can be individual words: *firstly, secondly, next, also, even, furthermore.* They can also be phrases: *moving on, having taken this into consideration, all things considered, that said.* Then there are the connectives used to close an argument: *to conclude, finally, in summary.*

It is the consistent use of appropriate structures, connectives and phrases that characterises good non-fiction writing. The teacher's job is to identify them and incorporate them into an enjoyable lesson.

What kind of lesson structure?

In order to balance prescription and creativity, the teacher's instructions and the child's independence, I have adopted the approach known as 'scaffolding' the lesson. The teacher demonstrates and models the skills necessary to achieve a successful lesson at the beginning of each paragraph or section, using good examples produced by her pupils to focus and encourage the rest of the class.

The teacher proceeds through the lesson, engaging the children in a short discussion at each stage, laced with examples and models, before setting them off to work independently. In this way, she can get away from what I have called 'Nike teaching', in which the teacher explains the entire lesson in the opening few minutes and sets the children off. This effectively says to the pupils: sink or swim. By breaking a lesson down into three or four bite-sized episodes, each lasting somewhere between ten and twenty minutes depending on the age and ability of the group, and each with its own objective, she makes the learning process more accessible. Teaching is purposeful and fast-paced and the child is supported throughout, avoiding the 'dribble-away' factor. This is when the pupils begin well but, through lack of direction or interest, lose interest and produce work that is well below their capabilities.

This approach works with all children and is particularly suited to those children who adopt visual and kinaesthetic approaches to learning, using what they see and what they do rather than what they hear. In short, it works with boys.

A sample lesson: writing instructions

Instructions are one of the easiest forms of non-fiction to teach. The key conventions are: headings, sub-headings, bullet points, the use of the colon and the use of imperative verbs in instructional sentences. How you teach them can make all the difference between an enjoyable experience which helps your pupils internalise the key pieces of information, and a dreary trudge through a series of stale facts that will not linger long in the mind.

I usually begin with a little anecdote, not because I like the sound of my own voice, though that is probably true, but because anecdotes enliven teaching. So here goes. My wife drives down the M62 to the Ikea store in Warrington. After a cup of coffee called something like a Grokkenflop, she chooses a wardrobe that has caught her eye. Unfortunately when it arrives *chez* Gibbons it comes in the form of a ready-to-assemble kit or flat-pack. We then have to read the instructions. These invariably break down into two sections. Firstly there is a list of the tools you will need:
• hammer
• screwdriver
• axe
• flame-thrower
• Valium!

Then there is a second section in which the writer directs you, in coherent instructional sentences, how to assemble your wardrobe. This might read something like this:

> Lay *out all the parts*. Collect *the tools you will need*. Attach *the back and side panels to the base and roof of the wardrobe*. Screw *in the hinges*. Secure *the door*. Screw *on the handle*. *If it is a complete mess*, attack *with the weapons and* take *the valium*.

The first part of the lesson, say ten or fifteen minutes, consists of demonstrating how to set out the instructions and how to present a list.

The teacher should demonstrate the title and first sub-title: *What you need*. She should then introduce the colon. Again, a little anecdote helps fix it in the children's mind. Tell them the colon is the creative midfield player of punctuation, the Paul Scholes, Steven Gerrard or David Beckham. It sets up the play, introducing the next bit of information. Don't tell anecdotes just the once. The children soon become familiar with a repeated story and internalise it. That's what patterned language in oral story-telling is all about.

Now we are ready to begin listing the items in our instructional booklet.

This is when you tell your class what we are writing about. The title is:

Vampire Slaying for Beginners

This too is introduced by a short anecdote.

> *Once upon a time a chap called Billy McDivvy left his local pub. Billy immediately fell over a body, and not just any body. This corpse was horribly pale and there were two puncture marks in its neck. Its body had been drained ... of blood!*
>
> *'Oh no,' Billy thought. 'We've got an outbreak of vampires.'*
>
> *Not being a terribly intelligent type, when Billy set about hunting down his vampire, his vampire-slaying kit was useless. He packed jelly babies, Johnson's baby powder and a feather duster. Not surprisingly, the vampire just laughed in his face, though the dust made him sneeze and the duster made him giggle.*

The teacher then says: 'You, class, are going to write some instructions for slaying the vampire. They have to be so clear and simple that even Billy can understand them.'

The teacher then gives the children about ten to fifteen minutes to draw up a list of items they need to slay a vampire. Brainstorming in groups is an effective strategy in this section of the lesson. With an able child acting as secretary, other children, hampered possibly by weaker spelling, can make a worthwhile contribution without having to worry too much about the secretarial element of writing. The brainstorming sheet then acts as a spelling resource.

The teacher then demonstrates that you bullet-point each item and only put one item on each line. Punctuation is not necessary while bullet-pointing. While the children are working she can point out that, if you use an adjective to qualify the noun in non-fiction, it generally comes *after* the noun. Sometimes you put it in parentheses.

The second section of the lesson, *What to do:*, is different. There are no bullet points. This time the children have to tell Billy in clear, simple instructional sentences what he has to do. The teacher can model several sentences as follows:

Find the cemetery. *Dig* down two metres. *Prise* open the coffin lid.

She will then point out the words in italics (they can be demonstrated by writing the imperative verbs on the whiteboard in red and continuing the rest of the sentence in blue). She can then make the grammatical point that imperative verbs are ones which give orders. Each sentence will start with one of these imperative verbs. Able children may be given extensions suggesting troubleshooting tips. The result is a clear, coherent and enjoyable piece of non-fiction writing.

Here is an example of children's work:

Vampire-slaying for beginners

By Chelsey Hodgson, Year 4

What to use:
- stakes, sharpened
- holy water
- cross
- crossbow
- garlic
- axe, sharp
- shovel, pointy
- mirror
- torch

What to do:
Put all the items in your vampire-slaying bag. Go to the graveyard and dig six feet down. Get your axe and put it on the grave. First you need to open it. Get your torch and see inside. Then chop the vampire up with your axe.

To show progression, here is an example from a child three years older in Year 6:

Instructions for an apprentice vampire-slayer

By George Murdoch, Year 6

What you need:
- one big, scary vampire (a weedy one called Spike is OK)
- one blunt stake (wooden)

- one rare steak (meaty – it's a hungry job)
- a crucifix (they always come in handy)
- two rounds of cheese and pickle sandwiches (bait)
- for an extra challenge, two zombies and an annoying helper (called Buffy, preferably)
- one spooky graveyard
- one full moon
- a coffin

What to do:

Firstly lay out the cheese and pickle sandwiches. Wait for your big, beefy but vulnerable vampire to eat the sandwich. Do some karate moves and show him your crucifix or stab him with your stake – the wooden one, stupid. Next wait for him to disappear. If he doesn't, get Buffy to maul him horribly and leave him whining piteously in the cemetery. Finally eat your steak but don't share it with your sidekick – it'll teach her a lesson.

If things go pear-shaped:

- if the vampire doesn't die, tell your mum he's spoiling your game and he'll apologize and die
- if you get scared (very likely) scream and run away – it's never failed Shaggy and Scooby Doo yet!

Helpful tips:

- always talk in an American accent
- wait for the theme tune to stop before laying your trap
- mangle your vampire horribly – Buffy'll get jealous

If anything goes wrong and you're not dead, call George – Transylvania.

Creative or functional?

Of course, this is not to say that there is no place for functional writing in the curriculum. There should be a balance. If the children can, however, play with conventions in an imaginative way, they are also more likely to be able to use them in more directly functional non-fiction activities of the kind which feature in national tests. It would seem sensible for teachers to do both and explicitly make the point that the children should develop an ability to distinguish when to go 'creative' and when to go 'functional.'

Here is a piece of work from a science lesson.

A fair test: bouncing balls

By Tom B., Year 3

What you need:
- tennis ball
- golf ball
- sponge ball
- metre rulers
- note pad

What you do:

You will need three children to do this investigation. One will hold a ball over the floor. One will measure how high it bounces. One will make notes. Hold each ball over the same part of the floor. Drop each ball from the same height. In this way you will be doing a fair test. Note how high each ball bounces against the ruler. Note it down.

The children can record this after discussing the fair test. After testing they will then note down their results in a table and draw some conclusions.

Revisiting instructions

Sometimes, in a crowded curriculum, teachers find it hard to visit a particular genre more than once. The temptation to buzz like a demented bee around the various topics you are expected to visit should be resisted. Teaching English as a kind of lucky dip isn't likely to work. It becomes a haphazard and purposeless process. If the pupils are to absorb the skills they need, some repetition is necessary. But it has to be meaningful and interesting repetition. One way to do this is to revisit the conventions and rules of a particular form in a slightly different way. As an example, the teacher could show that recipes follow exactly the same rules as instructions. The class could make a cake or flapjack in a D&T lesson and write it up, then, a few days later, undertake a creative writing lesson using the same format. It will refer back to earlier lessons on instructional writing and also visit it twice in writing recipes. This will help reinforce the skills learned.

A good way to focus the children in the creative writing follow-up is to take real ingredients as follows:

- 250 grammes of flour
- 50 mls of milk
- two eggs
- a dash of spice
- a cup of sugar
- a knob of butter

and so on. Write them up on a whiteboard in dry-wipe pen. Then simply rub out the words flour, milk, eggs, etc, leaving the measures on the board, and substitute with items related to the subject of the recipe, in this case Julius Caesar. Here is an example of a completed piece of work.

Recipe: how to bake a Julius Caesar cake

(Group work: Prescot County Primary School)

Ingredients:
- 250 grammes of Roman virtue
- 50 mls of Celtic blood
- two cruel eyes
- a dash of determination
- one purple toga
- one teaspoon of arrogance
- one suit of armour
- several books of military history
- a warning about the Ides of March

Method:
Take all the ingredients. Place them in a mixing bowl and mix thoroughly.
Pour into a baking tray and place in a hot oven for about sixty years.
Finally, throw away the warning about the Ides of March and ignore.
Garnish with a Shakespeare play and lots of fame.

Now you have your famous, and rather dead, Julius Caesar cake.

This enables the teacher to revisit the necessary skills without subjecting the class to a tedious diet of repetitive tasks. Hopefully, this example will demonstrate that, by consistently and thoroughly teaching the various forms of non-fiction, the teacher can establish a repertoire which pupils can employ to communicate in a wide range of situations. Short sequences of teaching can revisit the conventions and rules the children need to learn without boring them to death. Enjoyable lessons, laced with humour, and recognising children's interests and playfulness with language, can help pupils absorb the necessary skills in a child-friendly way.

Chapter 2

Speaking and listening as the basis for writing

Good quality writing does not emerge from nowhere. The wellspring of both reading and writing lies in speaking and listening. For us to become literate human beings, we must pass through a long, and far from easy, learning experience. Through listening we begin to internalise what a coherent unit of meaning sounds like. It is worth pointing out that most parents communicate this valuable information in a way that is anything but didactic. The 'basics' are conveyed through fun. Loving parents sing to their babies and toddlers. They recite nursery rhymes, fairy stories and traditional tales. They tell anecdotes and jokes. Children who become successful, literate adults have generally grown up playing with language, growing to love its elasticity and richness. They haven't been drilled and they haven't learned by rote.

This playfulness with language, this readiness to recognise its rules and conventions, then to test their limits, is at the heart of oracy and literacy. This is where Shakespeare gets a phrase like: 'but me no buts' (*The Comedy of Errors*). This is where Kenneth Williams got: 'Infamy, infamy, they've all got it in for me!'

The Primary National Strategy's Speaking and Listening guidance materials (DES/QCA Ref: DfES 0626-2003 G) are very helpful in encouraging children's oral skills. The materials identify four aspects of speaking and listening:

Speaking: being able to speak clearly and to develop and sustain ideas in talk.

Listening: developing active listening strategies and critical skills of analysis.

Group discussion and interaction: taking different roles in groups, making a range of contributions, and working collaboratively.

Drama: improvising and working in role, scripting and performing, and responding to performances.

Employing speaking and listening activities as a rehearsal for writing has many advantages:
* it helps address the 'oracy deficit' some children bring with them into school, enabling them to hear and reproduce coherent units of meaning
* it has a high interest level

- it establishes a resource which can be used to prepare for writing
- it permits children who have difficulties with writing but who are verbally articulate to succeed. Throughout this book you will find examples of group work produced by four or five children working collaboratively.

Speaking and listening should be an activity in itself. The rush to record has killed many a child's enthusiasm. What makes sense is to establish sequences of lessons which take the learner from speaking and listening through to reading and writing. How long these sequences last depends on the professional judgement of the teacher, but they should not be rushed. The distinctiveness of talk has to be recognised and valued. The first lesson, or lessons, should therefore be purely speaking and listening activities. Ensuing lessons should return to these same activities and build on their outcomes to establish the ground rules for writing lessons. As the materials state: 'Speaking and listening, reading and writing are interdependent. ... For many children, expressing ideas orally is easier than in writing, where it is more complicated to orchestrate all the necessary skills. The discipline of writing, which involves precision and clear articulation of meaning for a distant reader, aids clarity in oral communication too. Reading gives children models of language, and discussion of texts helps them to take such language into their own repertoire. So speaking and listening, reading and writing, are not only interdependent, but also mutually enhancing.'

An example

One area of writing many children find difficult is persuasive writing, particularly debates. A class could be asked to prepare a presentation on: 'Should parents be allowed to smack?'

The first lesson would be oral. Individual recording is not necessary. In the first section of the lesson the teacher could send the children off to brainstorm the arguments why children *should* be allowed to smack, e.g.:
- children need to learn discipline
- a little tap by a responsible adult can correct a child
- children need to know right from wrong

A secretary could list the arguments on a large piece of paper.

In the second section of the lesson the teacher could ask the children to brainstorm the arguments why children *should not* be allowed to smack, e.g.:
- smacking is violence and teaches children a bad lesson
- there are better ways of setting limits on bad behaviour
- it is illegal to hurt an adult so why should it be different with children?

The teacher can then help the children to structure their presentation, discussing what phrases the children might employ to improve their presentations. It might go like this:

1 Introduction
2 Arguments for the right to smack
3 Arguments against the right to smack
4 Conclusion

Each section could be rehearsed and a presentation prepared. It might go something like this:

Should parents be allowed to smack?

The right of parents to smack their children has been a subject of intense debate. In some countries smacking is banned. This is not true of the United Kingdom. Let's examine the arguments.

Supporters of the right to smack argue that children need to know the difference between right and wrong. Furthermore, they point to the need for discipline. They also argue that giving kids a 'little tap' does the child no harm.

Opponents of this view argue that parents should not be allowed to smack. They suggest that smacking only tells children that violence works and is a form of abuse. They further argue that there are better ways to discipline children: grounding, telling them off and denying them privileges. They finally argue that the law protects adults from violence, so why not children?

Of course, there are two sides to every story. Supporters of smacking point to the need for strong discipline. Their opponents stress the need to protect the child. In conclusion, I think that ... (here, the writer puts his or her viewpoint forward).

The sheets of useful phrases for the introduction and conclusion and the 'brainstorming' notes can then be kept. In a subsequent lesson, these sheets can be displayed, read through and form the basis of a written argument of debate.

In this way, speaking and listening activities can lead into writing activities. Having practised the skills required in a particular form of non-fiction writing orally, children tend to be far more confident when it comes down to completing the same tasks in written form.

Chapter 3

The lessons

How this section works

In the following pages you will find a series of sample lessons. They work like this:

- There is a short lesson plan based loosely on the *Grammar for Writing* materials.
- There are some notes on the structure of the lesson.
- There is a sample of children's work, with comments.
- There are some suggestions for follow-up.
- Finally, there is, where appropriate, a checklist or Toolbox of skills, conventions and useful phrases.

All these examples are taken from my own teaching. They were all completed in the standard fifty or sixty minute lesson. The stories have not been re-drafted. They are reproduced as they were given to me at the end of the lesson. I would suggest that these rough drafts could be put onto OHP transparencies and could be used to introduce a future lesson. Using an OHP pen the class teacher could demonstrate correction and redrafting of the original material.

I hope the lessons prove useful to a new generation of teachers.

Lesson 1

Writing instructions
How to ...

Lesson Plan

Objective: to notice differences in the style and structure of fiction and non-fiction.

Stimulus: show some examples of instructions to the children and discuss features (a simple set of notes from a construction or DIY kit, any kind of manual, even the little notes from a Kinder egg).

Sentence level: using bullet points and punctuating coherent sentences.

Shared writing: *Vampire-slaying for beginners* (See examples in Chapter 1).

Guided writing: Children write instructions: *How to recognise and destroy a werewolf.*

Structure of the lesson

Part 1

Write the title or heading clearly. On the next line, write the sub-title or sub-heading: *You will need*:

To introduce the items in this list you will need to use the creative midfield player of punctuation, the colon. It looks like this :

List all the things you will need to hunt your werewolf. Put one item on each line. Note that sometimes, for effect, if you qualify the noun with an adjective to describe it, in non-fiction the adjective might go after the noun, e.g.:

   bullet, *silver*

Alternatively, use parentheses.

   (silver) bullet
   bullet (silver)
   bullet (silver, of course!)

List alternatives and let the children experiment. At the heart of good writing lies the ability to play with language. Often there is no one right answer but a series of plausible options. Over-didactic teaching prevents children making choices and, without the ability to make choices, the available pathways to independent learning are closed off.

Part 2

OK, you have finished your list. This section doesn't use bullet points. The teacher models the first three sentences for the youngsters, explaining that they can begin with her example and carry on or do the whole thing in their own words. It depends on how confident they are feeling. The teacher puts the first word, the imperative verb, on the whiteboard in red pen and the rest of the sentence in black. By using different colours she draws attention to the use of imperative verbs at the start of the sentence, e.g.:

Shine your torch on the creature.

Remember to use a good finishing-off line, e.g.:

There, you've killed your first werewolf.

This is like the bow on a Christmas present, the sprinkle of chocolate on the cappuccino. It ties everything up.

Part 3

For the more able youngsters, they might want to add a last section:

Troubleshooting

They can use a sentence such as this:

Warning: your werewolf may not give in easily. If this happens …

They then describe their back-up plan if the monster fights back.

Examples of children's work ▬▬▬▬▬▬▬▬▬▬▬▬

How to recognise and destroy a werewolf

Robert G., Surrey, Year 6

What you need:
- videos of various Hollywood werewolf films
- photographs of dogs and timber wolves to aid identification
- rifle
- bullet (silver)

- dog whistle
- flashlight
- padded jacket
- earplugs

<u>What you do</u>:

Before you go hunting, watch the videos of werewolves. Compare the creature you see to the photos of dogs and wolves so you don't make a mistake. (NB. At night most dogs sleep. Werewolves don't!) As anyone will agree, no family wants to see their favourite poodle shot with a silver bullet! Put on your padded jacket. Remember, werewolves bite! Ready? Now, go down to the woods. Blow your dog whistle to attract the creature's attention. If you hear movement shine your torch in that direction. The moment you see the werewolf shoot it with your silver bullet. Be quick. He will be! There, you are now a werewolf-hunter, first class.

<u>Troubleshooting</u>:

Warning: your werewolf may not go quietly. If he turns out to be a cunning opponent hunt in pairs. You are more likely to trap him that way. Practise flanking manoeuvres at home. Try outflanking the pussy cat. Confusing a moggy is a first step to tracking down your first werewolf. Good hunting!

Comments

In this activity, Robert has revisited headings, sub-headings, bullet points and imperative verbs. The nature of the piece of writing encourages clear, well-demarcated sentence structures. It also gives the pupils plenty of scope for humour. Robert also uses questions and connectives to help the writing flow.

A follow up lesson might be something like this:

How to make a toy car from junk materials
How to make a puppet theatre
How to make the perfect den

Zanier examples might include:

How to build an IKEA teacher
Instructions on assembling a functioning parent
How to outwit an alien

Toolbox

Instructions must be clear. They split into two sections. There must be a heading and a sub-heading for each section.

The first section tells the reader what he or she will need. Use a colon and bullet points. There should only be one item on each line. A qualifying adjective tends to come after the noun in this kind of writing.

The second section, in coherent sentences using imperative verbs, tells the reader what to do. This should be systematic and the sentences should be short and direct.

Use a summing up phrase to finish off e.g. *There, you have completed your self-assembly wardrobe.*

Lesson 2

Writing Instructions

Recipes

Lesson Plan

  Objective: to notice differences in the style and structure of fiction and non-fiction.

  Stimulus: cookery book recipes.

  Sentence level: bullet pointing and sentence structure.

  Shared writing: demonstrate the structure of a conventional recipe.

  Guided writing: how to bake a Henry VIII cake.

Structure of the lesson

Part 1

Write a clear heading and the sub-heading *Ingredients*. After the sub-heading, use a colon to introduce the list. This is a list of all the things that go into the cake. The teacher should use a whiteboard and dry wipe pens. In discussion with the youngsters, she should list the ingredients of a conventional cake. What she is aiming for is a variety of measures (e.g. grams, litres, cupful, etc.). Once she has a long enough list, she can rub out jam, fruit, etc. and explain that this is no ordinary cake but a Henry VIII cake. The children should now substitute ingredients related to the life of this English king. Give the children several minutes to complete their list. They should bullet-point each item and put one item only on each line.

Part 2

This is the method. The children should tell their audience what to do and write in clear sentences, using imperative verbs at the beginning of each sentence. Demonstrate these verbs in a different-colour dry wipe pen from the rest of the sentence. Use a good concluding sentence.

Part 3

This is the decoration or garnish. Use something which refers to Henry VIII.

Examples of children's work

How to bake a Henry VIII cake

By Robyn Mitchell, Year 6

Ingredients:
- two bloodshot eyeballs
- six wives
- the odd divorce
- 250 g of excess weight
- one bushy beard
- a pair of tights
- a tsp of anger
- a dash of impatience
- a cup of diseases
- a tablespoon of Latin
- a drop of Spanish
- a jug of robes
- a carton of rich food
- a whole box of jailed monks
- a tsp of heads

Method:
Put all the ingredients into a large bowl. Mix well. Pop in a hot oven. Bake for 56 years.

Decoration:
Ice your cake with two divorces, two lost heads, one death and one survival. There, a delicious Henry VIII cake!

Recipe: how to bake a Henry VIII cake

By Ben Crawford, Year 6

Ingredients:
- two bloodshot eyeballs
- a Greensleeves song sheet
- the odd divorce

- 250 g of excess weight
- a beard
- one foot bigger than a football
- a pair of old smelly tights
- a dash of chicken legs
- a pinch of violence
- a jugful of fine clothes

Method:

Put all the ingredients into a bowl. Mix. Put in an oven for a million days.

Decoration:

Ice your cake with a crown and a medallion on top.

Comments

Both pieces of work by Year 6 pupils are in total control of the conventions and use them to make humorous comments about a historical figure. A piece of creative writing such as this both teaches the conventions of instructional writing and offers a better way of recording historical information than a dry-as-dust worksheet.

Here are some examples of follow-up activities:

How to make Dracula curry

By Lauren, Year 5

Ingredients:
- five jugfuls of evil
- two strips of flesh
- ten drops of blood
- sieve some horror
- crack in nine skeletons
- splash in one bat
- a pinch of terror
- three big eyeballs
- a smidgen of hearts
- a year's supply of cobwebs

Instructions:

Slam in the bat. Stir in the blood. Add in the eyeballs and the hearts. Sieve in the horror then throw in the flesh. Crack in the skeletons and pour on the terror. Add the cobwebs, horror and evil.

Garnish and keep cold for 8,000 years.

Recipe: a clean environment

By Lewis Sanderson, Year 3

Ingredients:
- a jugful of rainforest
- a litre of clean rivers
- 250g of litter bins
- a cup of unleaded petrol
- a kilo of street cleaners
- a sprinkle of polar ice caps
- a pinch of respect
- a touch of thought
- a packet of care

Method:

Put the ingredients in a bowl. Mix them. Pop the mixture in the oven. Bake it for months or even years. Decorate with an icing of love.

Suggestions

Using a recipe provides the children with one excellent way of presenting information. Done once a year, at varying levels of sophistication, such an activity in RE, PSHE, Geography or history would consolidate and develop the children's non fiction writing.

Here are some more ideas to think about:
- a rainforest stew
- a Chembakoli curry
- a Martin Luther King cake
- a Julius Caesar casserole
- a chemical formula for a successful democracy

Toolbox for instructional writing

It breaks down into two basic sections:

What you need / equipment / ingredients
This section is introduced by a colon and bullet-pointed. Bullet-pointing can be unpunctuated or use commas, semi colons or full stops. This depends on preference or the age and abilities of the youngsters.

What you do / method / instructions
This should be written in coherent, short, instructional sentences. Begin with an imperative verb, e.g. *Take, Cook, Fasten, Add*.

Lesson 3

Advertisements

Job ads

Lesson Plan

Objective: to write a piece of persuasive writing.

Stimulus: job advertisements in the local newspaper.

Sentence level: variety of punctuation.

Shared writing: demonstrate a job ad for a teacher, referring to TV ads.

Guided writing: write a job ad for a superhero.

Structure of the lesson

Part 1

One very effective strategy for persuading an audience is to ask them questions. This presents the reader with a challenge. The teacher asks the children to go into groups and brainstorm the kind of questions you would ask somebody who wants to become Superman. What would they need to be able to do? The teacher should model one or two questions on the board. Adding the question mark in a different question draws attention to punctuation in context.

Part 2

The teacher should pause the children and ask them to list the duties involved in the job, and the equipment needed. This will involve a list introduced by a colon, and bullet-pointed items.

Part 3

The last section should be the contact details of the employer, the postal address, email address and phone number. The teacher should go over how to set these out, modelling some examples on the board.

Examples of children's work

Vacancy: trainee Superman

By Matthew Garrett, Year 5

Have you got brains?

Do you hate villains?

Can you wear your underwear over your tights?

Can you eat Kryptonite?

If the answer is yes, this is the job for you.

Duties:
- saving the world before tea
- helping the police
- keeping your identity secret

Equipment you may need:
- costume
- X-ray eyes
- cape
- suitcase
- blue tights
- undies

Apply to:

Red Undies Inc.,

Blue Tights Grove,

Smallville,

USA.

Email: www.Superman.com

Tel: 0123 999 278.

Job advert: trainee Spiderman

By Jordan Chu, Year 4

Have you got good crime-fighting tactics? Do you like spiders? Can you fight villains? Can you swing from building to building? Then maybe you're the one for us.

Duties include:
- patrolling New York
- keeping a secret identity
- signing autographs
- wearing a mask

Useful equipment:
- suction pads
- web gunge
- clinging costume

If you think this is the job for you, apply to:
Superheroes Inc.,
Daring Street,
Marvel Town,
USA.
www.arachnid.com

Comments

Matthew and Jordan have produced pieces of writing which are confident, totally in control of the conventions and full of invention and irreverent humour. They work very well.

Here is another example of a job advertisement, this time for a trainee Santa Claus.

Job Advertisement: Trainee Santa required

By Nathan Fisher

Do you want to see the world?

Are you healthily heavy?

Do you like to make children happy?

Have you got a good appetite for mince pies?

Would you like to fly?

Would you like to work one day a year?

If the answer is yes, then read on.

Your duties will include:

- deliverance of presents
- reading several million letters
- looking after reindeer
- managing a team of elves
- eating lots of mince pies

Preference will be given to candidates with their own:

- black boots
- large sleigh
- hardwearing sack
- red suit

Pay and conditions:

- one penny for every ten presents delivered
- one penny docked for every present undelivered
- one hundred pound bonus if all presents delivered

Apply to:

101, Snowdrift Road, Penguin District, Lapland, PO Box 54-21.

Email: The_Christmases@yahoo.com

Suggestions

Writing a job advertisement for, for example, a historical or religious figure would be a good way for a pupil to demonstrate their knowledge of the individual in question.

Some examples might be:
• a Prime Minister
• a Roman Emperor
• a Viking warrior
• an Iceni queen
• a nurse in the Crimean war

Toolbox

Use a series of questions to hook the reader. Make sure you end each sentence with a question mark. Address the reader directly.

Put a clear sub-heading indicating the applicant's duties. Use a colon and bullet points to make a list.

Put a second sub-heading, listing the equipment needed for the job. Again use a colon and bullet points.

List, say, the pay and conditions. Again, colon and bullet points.

Finally, make sure there is a contact address. Set this out with each part of the address on a separate line. How does this relate to setting out a letter?

Lesson 4

Advertisements

Houses for sale

Lesson Plan

Objective: persuasive writing.

Stimulus: estate agent's brochures and the poem *Den to Let* by Gareth Owen.

Shared writing: an estate agent's report for Aladdin's lamp.

Guided writing: an estate agent's report for a haunted house.

Den to Let

By Gareth Owen

To let
One self-contained
Detached den.
Accommodation is compact
Measuring one yard square.
Ideal for two eight-year-olds
Plus one small dog
Or two cats
Or six gerbils.
Accommodation consists of:
One living-room
Which doubles as kitchen
Bedroom
Entrance-hall
Dining-room
Dungeon
Space capsule
Pirate boat
Covered wagon
Racing car
Palace
Aeroplane
Junk-room

And look-out post.
Property is southward facing
And can be found
Within a short walking distance
Of the back door
At bottom of garden.
Easily found in the dark
By following the smell of old cabbages and tea-bags.
Convenience escape routes
Past rubbish-dump
To Seager's Lane
Through hole in hedge
Or into next door's garden;
But beware of next door's rhinoceros
Who sometimes thinks he's a poodle.
Construction is
Sound corrugated iron
And roof doubles as shower
During rainy weather.
Being partially underground,
Den makes
A particularly effective hiding place
When in a state of war
With older sisters
Brothers
Angry neighbours
Or when you simply want to be alone.
Some repair work needed
To north wall
Where Mr Spence's foot came through
When planting turnips last Thursday.
With den go all contents
Including:
One carpet – very smelly.
One teapot – cracked
One woolly penguin –
No beak and only one wing
One unopened tin
Of sultana pud
One hundred and three Beanos

Dated 1983-1985
And four Rupert annuals.
Rent is free
The only payment being
That the new occupant
Should care for the den
In the manner to which it has become accustomed
And on long summer evenings
Heroic songs of days gone by
Should be loudly sung
So that old and glorious days will never be forgotten.

Reading this poem will encourage the children to think about the kind of language used in this style of writing. It evokes estate-agents-speak in a humorous way.

Structure of the lesson

Part 1

The children will all be familiar with *The Simpsons'* episode in which Marge becomes an estate agent. Mention it, and you will have instant recognition. Point out how language is used to hide faults. A tiny kitchen becomes 'snug.' Similarly, a house with a leaking roof becomes 'well ventilated.' The teacher can then show them a selection of estate agents' brochures.

Ask the pupils to get into groups. One child acts as secretary. They have a sheet of paper split into two columns. In the first they list the phrases used by estate agents to persuade us to buy. In the second they list any abbreviations and terms with which they are not familiar. The groups then bring their sheets to the plenary session to discuss and list phrases used by estate agents to persuade their customers. The teacher explains some terms and makes a 'master list' of phrases which will act as a toolbox.

Part 2

In the first section the children are asked to list the accommodation (rooms) in the haunted house. Stress that the humour of the activity generally works best if they understate the ghostly elements, playing a bit of a guessing game with the reader. Demonstrate that there are two ways to make a list. The children could either use a colon (:) and use bullet points, or a colon and items separated by commas. The teacher should remind them that there is no comma before the last item. Instead, they should end with 'and' and the last item. A good idea is to make lists in both ways in the course of the lesson to generate flexibility.

Part 3

The teacher should ask several children to share their first paragraph and point out what works especially well. The children can now list 'other interesting features' or some similar formulation. Share again.

Part 4

To complete the presentation, the children should describe the haunted house's location and neighbourhood and set a price. A brief discussion will throw up all sorts of ideas. The children should be reminded about possible connectives such as:

Finally
To conclude
In conclusion
In summary
Summing up

These are useful to tie up a piece of writing. Only by reading them out in context can you choose which one works best.

Examples of children's work

Jorgensen and Loftus: estate agents

For sale: an antique luxury house

By Eleanor Groves, Year 5

The accommodation in this adventurous property consists of: master bedroom, large kitchen, airy attic, spacious lounge and luxury lavatory.

Other interesting features can be found. For example, there are:

- fitted spirits in the lavatory
- trap doors in the master bedrooms
- bats in the attic
- giant snakes in the kitchen

The house is conveniently situated in Transylvania. The surrounding woods are full of werewolves and vampires.

Finally, the neighbours are the friendly Mr Ad and Mrs Dams, very friendly people.

Price: only £5.00, a snip!

Excellent value.

Haunted House to Let

By James Eastaway, Year 5

To let: one mansion with character.

Accommodation consists of: basement, room of doom, trap door, a huge pit, a moat filled with crocodiles, a dying room and a cavern.

The house has many unusual features. These include:
- moving staircases
- swords that swing themselves
- self-shooting arrows
- freaky people
- walking Tutankhamun
- flying pterodactyls
- piranhas in a tank

In addition, this desirable residence comes with many free accessories such as: starving crocodiles, organ, spell books, razor sharp swords, a million year old coffin and free bandages.

The price is a spooky £54,000.

For more details call: 289 8935.

Comments

Eleanor and James quickly absorb estate agents' language (character, desirable residence, conveniently situated). They structure their ads confidently, using colons, bullet points and commas. One interesting gender point: At first Eleanor seems almost apologetic about introducing the supernatural elements while James throws himself into it with gusto!

To extend this activity, the teacher could ask the children to include sections on transport, local schools and shops, etc.

Other similar activities might be related to history or geography:
- To let: mediaeval England
- For sale: a Brazilian rainforest

Toolbox

Begin with the phrase *To let* or *For sale*. Clearly indicate from the beginning the purpose of the piece of writing.

Indicate what the accommodation consists of. Use a colon and commas to make a list. Introduce the last item with *and*.

Indicate the features in the house. This time use the colon and bullet points to show you know more than one way to record a list.

Describe the location and neighbourhood.

Put a price on the house.

All the way through, stress the positive points of the house. Find a way of describing the drawbacks without putting off the buyer.

Some useful vocabulary:
this desirable residence
includes
consists of
features
all mod cons (modern conveniences)
compact
well-presented
convenient
with character
period features
bright
spacious
well-decorated
well-appointed
decorated to a high standard
close to all amenities

Lesson 5

Presenting information
A last will and testament

Lesson Plan

Objective: to write a non-chronological report.

Stimulus: Last will and testament of Alan Gibbons.

Sentence level: sentence structure and punctuation.

Shared writing: Last will and testament of ... (teacher's name).

Guided writing: Last will and testament of ... (child's name).

The basic form of a will might go something like this:

To whom it may concern.

On the death of John Smith, he will leave to his wife and family:
- his savings of £5,000
- his family home and all its contents
- his collection of portrait paintings
- his car
- his various belongings

Witnessed this day, August 1st, 2005 by Julia Cookson (solicitor).

Taking this basic form, it is possible to reflect on an individual's personality through the conventions. So:

Last will and testament of Alan Gibbons

To whom it may concern, anticipating a premature and gory death any day now, struck down by low flying teddy bears in Blackburn, Lancashire or overcome by a lethal attack of boredom during an episode of *Eastenders*, I hereby make the following provisions.
- I leave my priceless collection of Crewe Alexandra programmes to my wife.
- I leave my many books to schools with inadequate libraries.
- I leave my treasured Toyota Avensis to my eldest son on condition he is gentle with it.

I also make the following bequests:

- I bequeath my unique sense of humour to my family to remind them what they're missing.
- I bequeath my delightful singing voice to Aled Jones so he can carry on serenading The Snowman.
- Finally, I bequeath my love of peace to politicians everywhere.

I instruct that my ashes be strewn over the green plains of Cheshire so I can enjoy their beauty forever.

Witnessed this day, March 1st, 2005

by Muhammad Ali and Nelson Mandela.

Structure of the lesson

Part 1

The teacher should explain that a will and testament lists what a person wants done with their property after his or her death. The pupils can use the format to sum up their own worth and personality in the here and now.

The first short section of the lesson (say five minutes) is devoted to designing an interesting and idiosyncratic death, using the phrase:
To whom it may concern …

This will have to be modelled on the board and some ideas shared with the class.

Part 2

This consists of a series of sentences all beginning: *I leave …*

This is a useful exercise in forming coherent sentences. Again, modelling is important. Ask several children to explain one thing they would leave. The stress here is on clear self-expression. If necessary, the teacher can point out the essential components of the sentence such as noun and verb.

Part 3

Again, the stress is on coherent sentences, this time using the phrase: *I bequeath … .* There is only one difference in this section. Instead of leaving things or objects, the writer is now leaving qualities or abilities. This may be personality traits, sporting skills, or the ability to sing or dance.

Part 4

This final section is made up of two short sentences. First, the child chooses where they would have their ashes strewn or where they would be buried. It may be a sporting venue, a place they have visited and has some sentimental value, or a holiday destination they have enjoyed.

Finally, they choose a famous figure to be the witness to the will. This will have to be explained.

Examples of children's work

Last will and testament of Wendy Cheung

To whom it may concern.

Anticipating a premature death due to an overdose of cheesy soap operas, I instruct that my belongings be left as follows:

I leave all of the rubbish under my bed to my brother.

I leave my side of our bedroom to foreign exchange students with nowhere to live.

I leave my clothes to the whole cast of Emmerdale.

I leave all my comics and books to the sheep on the farm in Farm Road.

I leave all the money under my bed to the daddy-long-legs in the corner of the bathroom.

I further bequeath:

I bequeath my beautifully conditioned skin to the tortoises in Chester Zoo.

I bequeath my intelligence and knowledge to the chickens in the Big Brother House.

I bequeath my netball skills and sports ability to my Grandma.

I bequeath my angelic singing voice to my pet dog.

I instruct that my ashes be strewn over my old primary school so I can haunt it forever.

Witnessed this day, 25th July, by Elvis Presley.

Last will and testament of Nathan Fisher

To whom it may concern.

Anticipating a premature death due to grief over my goldfish being run over, I instruct that my belongings be left as follows:

- I leave my two guitars to my father, who can sell them to buy a banjo.
- I leave my CD player and various punk CDs to Liam.
- I also leave my bed to Liam who may sell them to buy a life.
- I leave my guitar picks to be distributed through my school so people may remember me by them.
- I leave my collection of mouldy receipts to the Oxfam shop in Wrexham because I like to help charity.

I further bequeath the following:
- I bequeath my huge brain to David Beckham.
- I bequeath my speed to McDonald's staff everywhere.
- I bequeath my life savings of twenty two pence to Cancer Research.
- I bequeath my sense of humour to Frank Skinner.

I instruct that my ashes be strewn in a jungle somewhere in the Deepest Amazon.

Witnessed this day, 25th July, by Billie-Joe Armstrong of Green Day.

Comments

Wendy and Nathan are in complete control of the form and use it to make some biting, satirical points.

The format could usefully be employed to put across historical facts e.g.:
- Last will and testament of Julius Caesar.
- Last will and testament of Mary Seacole.

Toolbox

Start with the phrase: *To whom it may concern.*

Phrases: *anticipating, expecting* meaning looking forward to.

Bullet-point the things or qualities you would leave. Start the list with a colon. Write one coherent sentence on each line.

When you choose a burial place use the phrase: *I instruct ….*

Choose a witness who will ensure the provisions are carried out.

Lesson 6

Persuasive writing
Brochure: The Ideal School

Note

The next few lessons cover similar skills and conventions in different ways. A good idea would be to assign each activity to a different year group in order to revisit the dynamics of such a piece of writing and reinforce the children's knowledge. They could do the simpler activities in Year 4 or 5 and the more complex and demanding in Year 6, 7 or 8. In order to consolidate children's knowledge some repetition is necessary, but it can be done in an interesting and stimulating way.

Lesson Plan

Objective:	to write persuasively.
Stimulus:	clips of TV presenters, brochures.
Sentence level:	second person, addressing the reader directly.
Shared writing:	a brochure for a real school.
Guided writing:	a brochure for the ideal school.

Structure of the lesson

Part 1

To set the scene it may be worth showing one or two TV clips of presenters at work. The likes of Lloyd Grossman in *Through the Keyhole* or the presenters of *A Place in the Sun* might be worth using. What we are looking at is how the presenter addresses the viewer directly, using the second person: *Look at, Note, Enjoy, Let's see,* etc. This is all about drawing the viewer or reader in.

The children can then be sent off in groups to look at a series of brochures. For the purposes of this lesson, school and college prospectuses are ideal. The pupils are looking for the phrases writers use to 'sell' their establishment to prospective parents and students. This will form the basis of the toolbox of useful phrases.

Part 2

The teacher should now bring the pupils back together into a plenary session and discuss which phrases the writer uses to address the reader directly and build a relationship with them. She can model a short version of a prospectus for their own school, drawing on their ideas. It might go something like this:

St Thomas' Primary

Welcome to St Thomas' Primary.

Enter the school from Wood Lane, a quiet residential road. Being a through road, there is little congestion here, making it easy to drop off the children. The lay by in front of the school means you can pull off the road in safety.

As you walk through the school grounds pause for a moment to take in the outside environment. There are early years and junior playgrounds with safe, recently-installed play equipment. The school field offers ample room for a wide range of sporting activities.

On the way into the school itself you need to identify yourself to the school secretary. Your child's security is our concern. The foyer is bright and spacious with a seating area where you can wait to be greeted.

Let's move on to the learning environment itself. The hall doubles as an assembly hall and indoor gymnasium. The classrooms are spacious and well-furnished. Each classroom is fitted with an interactive whiteboard.

From the welcoming and colourful nursery through to the Year Six classroom, the school is bright and comfortable. The newly-refurbished library is well-stocked with recent fiction, poetry and non-fiction. There is also a networked Information Technology suite. Finally, there is a designated TV room.

Happy so far? To build community links there is also a family room. This is where you will have a coffee and a chat after your child's sharing assembly. You never know, you may come here if you join our thriving Parent Teacher Association.

So that is our school community. We aim to provide a good quality education, delivering good academic and sporting results without neglecting the other aspects of a child's development.

We look forward to you joining us.

Part 3

The teacher should now introduce the subject they are going to write about: Welcome to the Ideal School. For younger pupils she may need to explain that this is the best school you can imagine. They are going to use the phrases they have identified to walk their reader through the Ideal School and show the reader what's good about it.

In the first paragraph they should welcome the reader and talk about their initial impressions as they enter the school grounds. What would the gates be like, the car park, the grounds? They should leave sport and leisure until later.

Part 4

This paragraph should introduce the reader to the learning environment. What would the uniforms be like? What about the classrooms and corridors? Don't forget the classroom equipment. Give these some thought too:
- the library
- audio visual rooms
- displays
- carpets/blinds/etc., the fittings and fixtures

Part 5

This paragraph could explore the sport and leisure factilities. Consider these:
- indoor and outdoor sports facilities
- coffee bars and 'chill out' areas
- canteen, or should that be restaurant

Part 6

Finally, once the children have guided their reader round the ideal school, remembering to use those phrases to address the reader directly, we will need a good summing up paragraph. This can be short. It may mention academic standards before hitting the reader with a good closing sentence. Something like this might do the trick: 'You want the school of tomorrow? Here it is today!'

Note how the punctuation reinforces the message.

Examples of children's work ▮▮▮▮▮▮▮▮▮▮▮▮▮▮▮▮▮▮▮▮▮▮

The Ideal School

By Faye (Huyton with Roby CE)

Welcome to the Ideal School. Drive through our voice-activated automatic safety gates. Pull up in our well-maintained executive car park. You will have your own parking bay watched by our high-tech CCTV cameras. Moving on, observe our beautiful, manicured lawns on which your child will enjoy playing. Look at the well-stocked flower beds and take a look at our fabulous fountains. If you've got a minute, take a seat in our bird-watching area and you might also see our wild flower meadows. Breathe in the fragrances of the gardens as you wander around.

Impressed? You haven't seen anything yet! Walk through our air-conditioned building. As you may have noticed, our children are wearing their smart Armani uniforms, plus they are working on their own personalised lap-top computers. If they are tired they can stop off to sip a latte in our coffee bar. If your child prefers something else, it will be provided. As you may have already noticed our classrooms are circular which gives our teachers easy access to the children.

But it's not all hard work! Take a look at some of our excellent sport and leisure facilities:

- boating and canoeing lakes
- floodlit football pitches
- Olympic-style swimming pools, inside and out
- hot sauna
- bubbly Jacuzzi

Our school will be the best your school will find, with excellent results so if you want to come to this school, they're welcome!

Comments ▮▮▮▮▮▮▮▮▮▮▮▮▮▮▮▮▮▮▮▮▮▮▮▮▮▮▮▮▮▮▮▮▮▮

This piece of work demonstrates how non-fiction writing can be fun. These young writers are using specific conventions they have drawn from brochures they have examined but they are also playing with language. Because they are given time to investigate and test the conventions, they come up with inventive, interesting work. If they can produce brochures of this quality, writing something more 'functional' should prove relatively easy.

You could follow up this activity by asking the children to write a similar piece about the Ideal Holiday Resort. Having visited the conventions once they should have absorbed much of the terminology they will employ.

Part 1

Describe flying into the resort. What are the first impressions of the palm-fringed beaches, the town, the surroundings from the vantage point of your aeroplane?

Part 2

Describe the hotel. What facilities does it have? What is the service like? Is it friendly?

Part 3

Describe the excursions, the main theme parks. The children can be as inventive as they like here. There could be a Homer Simpson World, a Spiderman World, etc.

Part 4

Sum up the holiday resort with a catchy phrase.

Toolbox

Start with: *Welcome to ...*

Use phrases to address the reader directly. Here are some examples:
See ...
Look at ...
Observe ...
Explore ...
Investigate ...
Enjoy ...
Pause for a moment by ...
Walk along ...
Picture yourself ...
Imagine ...
This is the ...

Use questions:
Fancy a rest? Then …
Want to go for a swim? Try our pool.
Peckish? Why not pop into our restaurant?
Time to chill out? Our coffee bar is the obvious place to go.
Impressed? You've seen nothing yet!

When you come to the last paragraph, don't forget the appropriate connectives:
Finally …
To sum up …
In summary …
In conclusion …
To conclude …

Close the piece with a catchy phrase:
- *There you are. It was quite a ride, wasn't it?*
- *That's journey's end. Come back soon.*
- *You want the school of tomorrow? Here it is today!*
- *You want traditional values in a modern setting? This is the place for you!*

Lesson 7

Descriptive writing
A Beginner's Guide to the Vikings in Britain

Lesson Plan

Objective: descriptive writing.

Stimulus: TV holiday programmes, travel brochures, information books about Vikings.

Sentence level: second person, addressing the reader directly. Clear, coherent sentences.

Shared writing: a modelled example.

Guided writing: children write their own guide to the Vikings in Britain.

Structure of the lesson

Part 1

The teacher should discuss with the children how writers and presenters involve the reader, and list some of the strategies they use:
• using an eye-catching opening line
• setting the tone of the piece of writing early, looking forward to the issues involved
• addressing the reader directly with phrases like *Let's, Just consider, Imagine,* etc.
• using bullet points to list features to be considered

The first paragraph describes the Vikings on their way across the sea to Britain. What would they be doing? Use your study of the topic. The teacher might ask the pupils to imagine they are flying over the Viking longboat with a TV camera strapped to them. Many documentaries and Hollywood movies use this technique. See *West Side Story, Enemy of the State,* etc., even *The Sound of Music*.

Part 2

This paragraph might describe the Vikings invading Lindisfarne or some other part of Britain. The children should imagine what they would look and sound like, and what they would actually be doing.

Part 3

This paragraph needs a linking sentence, for example: But it isn't all battles. The pupils should then describe the domestic life of the Vikings. The sentences can now be quite simple, describing what they are doing.

Part 4

It might be an idea to start this paragraph with a complex sentence: *But, late at night, what do they fear?*

This is teaching grammar for a purpose, grammar in context. There is a main clause: *But, what do they fear?* There is a subordinate clause: *late at night.* The teacher could demonstrate how they go together with the appropriate punctuation, two commas, and there you go, a complex sentence complete with subordinate clause. In this section they could explore the Vikings' beliefs.

Part 5

The teacher can now discuss with their students what kind of phrase could sum up the piece of writing effectively.

Examples of children's work

A beginner's guide to the Vikings

By Samantha Regan, Year 6

Let's follow the dragon ship across the North Sea. Look at the Vikings. They look vicious with their big, long beards and helmets. They are cleaning their swords with cloths, making them dazzle in the sun. They are planning their next attack and going on about how great they are at fighting. They are snuggled up in their cloaks to keep warm. They are drinking mead out of their drinking horns. Hear the waves bash against the boat as they row.

Look, they are coming ashore. They leap out of the longship and charge over to the monastery. Don't they look fierce? Hear them scream and shout as they attack the monks. Their swords, axes, spears and shields are clashing against doors and altars. They are stealing coins, jewellery and paintings.

But it isn't all battles. It's time we had a look at the Vikings' home life. They live in wooden huts with thatched roofs. They are cooking fish upon their fires. The children are playing pretend fighting with wooden swords.

But, late at night, what do they fear? They pray to Thor, God of thunder and Odin the one-eyed King of the Gods with his two ravens, Memory and Thought.

So that is our Viking tour. I hope you enjoyed the trip!

A beginner's guide to the Vikings

By Meghan Bruder

Let's follow the dragon ships across the North Sea. Look at the Vikings. See the vicious creatures sharpening their swords. Hear them roaring with laughter. Watch the sun glistening on their shining armour. Now listen to the oars splashing in the gleaming blue sea. Watch them drinking out of their horns of mead. Can you hear the horses' hooves on the wooden deck. Listen to the wind cracking in the sail.

Look, they have landed on a beach not that far from the monastery. Let's see what happens. Can you see them attacking the monastery? Aren't they terrifying? Listen, that's their footsteps coming closer. They are about to have a battle. Just watch those puddles of blood forming on the ground. They are taking away money, artefacts, paintings and even some jewellery.

But it isn't all battles. It's time we had a look at their home life. Smell the smoke coming from the fire. See the women weaving and cooking. Watch the children playing with their wooden weapons. Some women are cooking fish over the hot stoves.

But, late at night, comfortable in their beds, what do they fear? Maybe they are praying to Thor, the god of thunder for success in battle. Maybe they are praying to Odin for happiness in their and their families' lives.

So there it is, the end of our Viking tour. I hope you enjoyed it!

Comments

These two pieces of work present information about the Vikings in a pacey and effective way. They address the reader directly and employ connectives to keep the flow going. As a means of conveying historical knowledge it is more satisfying than a worksheet or a flat list of historical facts. Watch somebody like Simon Schama or David Starkey in action and you will see a more sophisticated, adult version of the same dynamic.

Here is an example of children's work using a similar approach.

A guide to ancient Egypt , Year 5

Fly into the land of Egypt across a glistening aquamarine sea. Now look at the golden sands. See the great Nile. Note the waving palm trees. There are camels wandering across the unspoiled sands. See the scaly green crocodiles basking on the river bank under a blazing sun.

Now let's go deeper inland and see the things that Egypt is famous for. Here you will find the pyramids. The Valley of the Kings is to the left. Imagine how many slaves must have died in the building of the pyramids and the Sphinx. Ready to go on? Let's explore the inside. There is a sarcophagus and hieroglyphics. There are scorpions on the floor. Do you think a mummy might come out of that sarcophagus?

But what about the lives of ordinary Egyptians? Here they are collecting water in pots at the village well and bringing it back to their flat-roofed home to store. At home there are seven rooms altogether:

- cellar
- food store
- kitchen
- living room
- bedroom
- staircase
- rooftop shelter

Sometimes when it is hot they sleep under a shelter on the roof.

Have you enjoyed yourself in Ancient Egypt? I hope you had fun on your tour. Come back any time!

This approach could convey information in a range of humanities topics.

Toolbox

Use a 'bird's eye view' to start the journey through the time or place you are examining.

Address the reader directly:

- *Look at ...*
- *Observe ...*
- *Listen to ...*
- *Hear ...*
- *There is/there are ...*
- *Approach ...*

As you continue the piece of writing, consider connectives:

- *now ...*
- *next ...*
- *moving on ...*
- *Oh, and here is ...*

You might want to bullet point some of the things you see or hear.

Choose good summing up phrases:

- *So that concludes ...*
- *We're at journey's end ...*
- *Finally, ...*
- *OK, that's our trip ...*
- *I hope you enjoyed it ...*
- *Come again ...*

Lesson 8

Presenting information in an imaginative way
A school as a menagerie

Lesson Plan

Objective: presenting information.

Stimulus: the poem 'School Creatures' by Gervaise Phinn.

Sentence level: second person, addressing the reader directly.
Coherent sentences.

Shared writing: teacher models first paragraph.

Guided writing: children write an introduction to the school jungle.

School creatures
Gervaise Phinn

Mrs Price isn't nice,
Her tiger eyes they burn like ice.
Mr Ryan, hard as iron
Stalks the classroom like a lion.
Mrs Drew, little shrew,
Very nervous, very new.
Mr Ash, walrus tash,
Brings us all out in a rash.
Dr Gee, can barely see,
A little furry mole is he.
Mrs Page, in a rage,
Like an elephant in a cage.
Mr Brass, silly ass,
Plays the fool in every class.
Albert Baker, school caretaker,
Dangerous as an alligator.
But Mrs Meacher, our headteacher
Is a most delightful creature.

Structure of the lesson

Part 1

Read the children the poem and discuss how the poet describes the teachers as if they were wild creatures. Introduce the task. The children are going to describe their own school community as if it were a menagerie. Some children may need reminding that this has to be in the best of all possible taste! Explain that calling somebody a rat or a pig won't go down too well. There is a big difference between mischievous good humour and rudeness.

In the first paragraph the children can describe the caretaker. What creature will best sum them up? Describe the way it behaves. Use the tactic of addressing the reader directly.

Part 2

Describe the secretary in the same way. How can we describe her job, relating it to an animal? Brainstorming is a good way of gathering ideas. Could we use questioning in this section to involve the reader?

Part 3

Do the same for the head teacher and deputy head teacher. How can we show their status? What animal would be dominant? How would they behave?

Part 4

Finally, introduce the children and choose a good summing up sentence.

Examples of children's work

The Maryville Jungle

By Sam Humphries, Year 5

We approach through an infested sea. A huge shark creeps around the moat of Maryville School. The white caretaker shark searches for litter and rubbish. The gobbling jaws scoop up rubbish like a dustpan and brush. Quietly, the shark prowls like a cat and moves like a cheetah. Do not stare at the creature. If you *do*, <u>beware!</u>

    Let's go further through the jungle. What's that? Oh, it's Mrs Crawley the secretary bird, collecting up registers and pecking away at the computer. Letters are being collected while she squawks hello and goodbye to teachers and parents alike. Her wings are flapping vigorously, her beak clenching, clipboards colliding, paper wiggling.

Dare you go on? No? Well, I'll just have to force you. Soon, Mrs Fletcher will be blowing on her clarinet, a songbird. She flies about pecking notes. Further in the undergrowth, Mr Jorgensen, the school orang utan, swings through the office trees. His company has branches everywhere. So does his office. The maze of his office is hard to complete.

Suddenly, the lioness comes and has been sheltering in Mrs Loftus' gloomy bat cave. Mrs Carson, the school lioness, roars across the maze out of Mr Jorgensen's office. This roar bellows out and all creatures must flee apart from the King orang utan. Mrs Loftus' wings fly around and she hangs from Mrs Crawley's perch (upside down, obviously!)

Finally, hear the stampede of four hundred rhinoceroses charging around school gathering brain cells. Chaos and havoc now roam the school.

Comments

This is a very accomplished piece of writing. Again, it shows how, with a little bit of imagination, a young writer can use non-fiction formats, skills and conventions to write very creatively. Sam uses the tricks of the trade accumulated in the kind of writing exhibited in the previous two chapters to write something very exciting and refreshing to read.

Suggestions

- A report on a Big Brother household featuring a cast of historical characters (Julius Caesar, Mary Seacole, Henry VIII, Guy Fawkes, Churchill, Elizabeth 1)
- A report on a Big Brother household featuring a cast of storybook characters (Big Bad Wolf, Little Red Riding Hood, Dracula, Charlie Bucket, Harry Potter, Voldemort)

Toolbox

As Lesson 6.

Lesson 9

Autobiography

Lesson Plan

Objective: to write an autobiography.

Stimulus: a short autobiography written by the teacher.

Sentence level: complex sentences.

Shared writing: teacher's opening paragraph.

Guided writing: children write their own autobiographies.

N.B. Given the difficult circumstances of some children's lives, this may require the exercise of professional judgement, omitting sensitive areas of the child's life.

Structure of the lesson

Part 1

It is good practice for the teacher to write herself. It shows the children that she is a writer and helps convince them that they can be writers. She can use her own simple autobiographical piece as a model for the class.

Part 2

Having modelled an opening paragraph, the teacher can now give examples of the kinds of phrases which catch the reader's attention. She should show how to start from the very first line. She should then look at the various phrases which address the reader directly and draw them into the piece of writing. Questions work quite effectively too. The young writers should now describe their early years before starting school.

Part 3

Having explored the early years, the children should now look at such experiences as first day at school, school friends, days out, etc. It helps to concentrate on anticipation. How did they feel on their first day? What had people told them about school? Many young children make a chronological list of events. Asking them to concentrate how they felt on the way to school, or what they thought when they first met a particular friend, or how they felt boarding the bus to a school trip, adds quality to the writing and resists the temptation to rush through it.

Part 4

This paragraph could deal with where the children are now, their interests, their hopes for the future. Open teacher questioning usually focuses the children on the kind of information they should include. How do you see yourself as an adult? Where will you live? What kind of job will you have? Will you have a family of your own? Can you think of one ambition you would like to fulfil? As ever, they should finish with a good closing line.

Examples of children's work

Autobiography of Sian Edwards

A cry rang out down the corridor at St Asaph Hospital. I was in the world.

When I was about two years old my mum and dad took me to a gymnastics club just around the corner from my house. The first thing I heard and saw was my coach Ernie's booming voice telling everyone to be quiet or, as he put it, 'Shut up!' He had a big, fluffy moustache and brown hair with lots of little, grey hairs. He also had a big beer belly. That's what he called it as he tapped it ferociously. He also smoked a bit too much.

Let me take you back a year to just before I was one. That day my dad was sitting filming me like most parents probably do. Sitting there just by his foot, I bit it as hard as I could. Having just a few teeth it probably didn't hurt that much but my dad screamed his head off: 'Aaaargh!'

Anyway, I grew up fast, my dad going to work every day and me going to school, so now I'm in High School. I'll be in Year 8 in five weeks. Wow!

When I'm older I want to be an Olympic gymnast but I don't think I'll get there so I want to be a dance teacher, or a famous violin player like Bond, or maybe a pop singer. I'm not going to worry about that at the moment because I like school. I'm quite happy as I am.

So my name is Sian Marie Edwards and my initials spell out S.M.E like Smee of Peter Pan fame. I am a Sagittarius. As a young child I wanted to be a ballet dancer. Though I don't know why, my favourite TV show is Charmed on Channel 5 every Saturday, 6.50pm. Can you tell? Finally, my most treasured possessions are my mum and dad.

Comments

Sian's autobiography starts with a telling opening line. She orders the material confidently. As an example, she doesn't always follow a strict chronological order, instead organising her ideas by key moments, using the phrase: *Let me take you back.*

Toolbox

See Lesson 11.

Lesson 10

Biography
Alan Gibbons

Lesson Plan

Objective:	to write a biography.
Stimulus:	interview with Alan Gibbons.
Sentence level:	complex sentences.
Shared writing:	a model opening paragraph about a different writer.
Guided writing:	a biography of Alan Gibbons.

An interview with Alan Gibbons

Tell me about your early years.

I was born in 1953 in Warrington and grew up in the Cheshire countryside. My mum was a housewife at that time and my dad worked as a farm labourer. We lived in a tied cottage, a house owned by the farmer. When I was very young my dad had a terrible accident and ended up in hospital with a badly broken ankle. I can remember Mum and I spending a few days at my Gran's. Because of Dad's injury, we had to move to Crewe, where he got a factory job.

Was it easy to settle into your new school?

It took a while. Early on a few boys followed me around picking on me. One time I got shoved into a hedge. I was a bit scared of some of the teachers. They could shout a bit and occasionally they would throw things!

What sort of books did you enjoy?

I loved adventure stories and the Bobbsey Twins. I also loved myths and legends.

What jobs did you do?

I couldn't settle after school. I did all sorts of jobs. I worked in a tea factory. I did a spell as a boating lake attendant. I did welfare rights advice. Finally, I became a primary school teacher.

So where did the writing come from?

I'd always loved reading. When I became a teacher I used stories to win over my class and get them interested in reading and writing. A college teacher called Waltraud Boxall encouraged me to send off my stories.

Did success come quickly?

It depends what you call success. Getting published itself is a step forward. My first two books were *Pig* and *Our Peculiar Neighbour*. My first real success was probably *Shadow of the Minotaur* which won a Blue Peter Book Award. I've won two other awards.

Do you have any children?

Yes, four. I live with my wife Pauline and my kids Joe, Robbie, Megan and Rachel in Liverpool.

Do you write every day?

Yes, most days, for about two hours a day.

Extra sources and research

This interview can be supplemented by looking at the author's website: www.alangibbons.com

The children could also find other information by using a search engine like Google to look up Alan Gibbons.

There is a copy of Authorzone featuring an interview with Alan Gibbons from: www.peters-books.co.uk/contact.htm

In this way, they would do original research before embarking on the writing itself.

Structure of the lesson

Part 1

The teacher could demonstrate from a biography of, say, Charles Dickens, how biographers draw out general judgements from a life story, e.g. *It was Charles' experiences at the blacking factory that coloured his view of childhood.*

She could also demonstrate complex sentences, e.g. *Charles, seeing his older sister doing so well, must have wondered why he was doing such a dead end job.* By demonstrating the subordinate clause 'seeing his older sister doing so well', the teacher can distinguish it from the main clause.

She could finally model the use of phrases that address the reader directly, e.g.:
* *You can just imagine ...*
* *Picture Charles in his blacking factory ...*
* *What could he have felt?*
* *Try putting yourself in his shoes. How did he feel?*

Part 2

The teacher can now look at the section of the interview dealing with the studied author's early years and suggest how the children might summarise the details. She could ask the children to brainstorm some sample sentences and share them with the class. The key here is to highlight sentences that are incisive and will catch the reader's attention.

Part 3

The teacher can read some sample opening paragraphs and ask the children for their comments. What works well? Now the children can go on to write about the author's school days, not forgetting to draw out turning points or key moments. Phrases such these might help:
- *A key turning point was when …*
- *A major crossroads occurred when …*
- *An influential figure in X's life was …*

Part 4

This should chronicle the adult years, possibly drawing out the ways in which the adult was formed by the child. It should also conclude with a telling closing line, for example:
- *It was that early love of reading that led to a career as a writer.*
- *Those early experiences led to a life as a writer. Since finding his niche, X has not looked back.*

Examples of children's work

Biography of Alan Gibbons

By Wendy Cheung

The themes of Alan Gibbons' books were determined by his early childhood. He was born in 1958 and lived in a tied cottage in the Cheshire countryside. He spent the long summer days playing with his pet dog, Wendy, and making the most of the country. This all came to a stop when he was little. His father was a farm labourer and had a terrible accident which nearly cost him his foot. He was in hospital for five months and during that time Alan and his mother had to move to Crewe to live with his grandmother. He had to start a new school. The old village school in the countryside only taught 23 children. You can just imagine how nervous he felt when he started the new 400-pupil school in the city!

In and out of school, he was bullied by three older and bigger boys. They picked on him for his love of books and reading. They pushed him into the same hedge every day after school. He had to hide the scratches and scrapes from his mum. The bullying didn't just come from the pupils. Two teachers especially noticed him. One would throw chalk. The other threw board dusters at him, for fidgeting.

Alan's adventure and myth stories are influenced by his own reading experiences. He was told myths and legend stories as a child and had many adventures with his friends, acting them out.

As a young man, Alan didn't know what to do with his life. He had many strange jobs such as working in a tea-bag factory, being a boating-lake attendant and a welfare advice worker. He started work as a primary school teacher. A teacher there called Mrs Boxall encouraged Alan to send off a story for publishing after seeing him tell his class a story called 'Anansi and the Crocodile'. Pig was a success and just the first of Alan's many books. Pig was published when Alan was 38 and, even now, when he is older and has made up his mind to be a professional writer, he has still got lots more books to come. One of his best books Shadow of the Minotaur recently won a Blue Peter Book Award. He lives in Liverpool with his wife and four children and writes for two hours a day. He also teaches. He is a big inspiration to other young writers.

Comments

Wendy's biographical piece is mature and assured. She has a good understanding of the material and structures it well. There are some telling phrases e.g.:

'The themes of Alan Gibbons' books are determined by his early childhood.'

'You can just imagine how nervous he felt when he started the new 400-pupil school in the city!'

'He had to hide the scratches and the scrapes from his mum.'

Suggestions

Other subjects for biographical writing might be:
• J.K.Rowling
• Jacqueline Wilson
• Malorie Blackman
• Robert Swindells
• Roald Dahl
• Anthony Horowitz

Indeed, any visiting author or any writer chosen for study would be good. To this end 'Author zone' from Peter's Booksellers is indispensable. There are also a number of good biographies of children's authors on the market in easy-read formats.

In addition to authors, there are many subjects in the humanities:
• Martin Luther King
• Mother Theresa of Calcutta
• Mary Seacole
• Julius Caesar
• Isambard Kingdom Brunel
• Winston Churchill

Toolbox

See Lesson 11.

Lesson 11

Biography
Thor, the Thunder God

Lesson Plan

Objective:	to write a biography.
Stimulus:	topic books about the Vikings.
Sentence level:	sentence structure.
Shared writing:	opening paragraph of the biography.
Guided writing:	complete the biography.

Structure of the lesson

Part 1

The teacher could ask the children to go into groups and browse topic books about the Vikings. If they are writing about a mythical or story book character they can take certain liberties, inventing parts of the person's childhood, etc. Once the basic research is done, one child could act as secretary and take notes for the group. These could be shared in a short plenary session. The teacher could make a 'master list' of main points about Thor.

Part 2

The teacher should model good opening lines. The aim is not to start chronologically, but to capture the reader's attention. The rest of the paragraph should describe Thor's early life, family, pets, etc. Short, coherent sentences work best.

Part 3

The next paragraph should describe Thor's schooldays. Who were his friends? Who did he not get on with? What were his favourite subjects?

Part 4

In the final paragraph, the children could describe Thor's adult years. The biography should end with a good closing line, summarising his life or abilities.

Examples of children's work ▐▬▬▬▬▬▬▬▬▬▬▬▬▬

Thor, the thunder god

Unnamed boy, Year 4, Huyton School

A cry rang out down the corridors of Asgard Hospital. Thor was born. His dad, Odin, was King of the gods. His mum, Frigg, was Queen. When Thor was eight years old he went to war for the first time. He killed the most powerful dragon in the world with his rattle. He was so powerful he needed a special dummy made out of titanium.

When he was five Thor started school at Valhalla County Primary. He made one enemy, a boy called Loki. Loki was his worst nightmare. When Thor was in fourth year he got a girlfriend called Sif. She had long, golden hair. Thor was very good at metalwork. He was born with a hammer in his hand and has never stopped using it since.

Finally, Thor died at Ragnarok, the battle at the end of the world, poisoned by a giant serpent. That was the end of Thor, one of the best-loved of all the Norse gods.

Dracula

By Adam Hilton, Year 5

This is the true, and horrible, tale of Count Dracula. As a baby, he played with toy bats. He used to go down to the cemetery to play with Frankenstein and his mummy. He liked nothing better in the morning than a nice glass of warm blood.

Then, one fine, dark night, when the lightning flashed and the thunder crashed, he started Beast-enders Primary School. At the age of ten he got suspended for eating the head teacher, or should we say headless teacher?

But life didn't turn out a dead-bunch of roses. He lived in a dark, gloomy castle with Igor, his best friend. He was short of friends because he'd eaten them all. He liked everything except stake (not a spelling mistake). He also had a life-long argument with Van Helsing. I hope you liked the biography of ... MY DAD!!!

Comments

The short biography of Thor begins with a striking opening and continues crisply and coherently. There are some amusing touches, such as the dummy made of titanium. For a boy in Year 4 this is a very controlled and accomplished piece of work.

In his biography of Dracula, Adam uses the form very well to demonstrate a mischievous sense of humour. He exhibits a good control of subordinate clauses and punctuation and uses both to produce a quirky, funny and effective piece of writing.

Naturally, this sort of writing also applies to straight biographical writing. Here is an example.

Biography of Julius Caesar

Peter, Year 5

Julius Caesar was one of the world's greatest generals. He was probably the best known Roman of them all.

He was born in 100BC to a well-known Roman family. His father died when he was a teenager. When he became a soldier he was very brave. He saved the life of a citizen in battle.

Once, on his way to Greece, he was kidnapped by pirates. He told them he would be back to deal with them. He was true to his word and led a raid on them. He had their throats cut for kidnapping him. This shows how ruthless he was.

Soon he became a politician and general. When he was in his forties he went to Gaul for nine years and conquered many tribes. He made a big reputation for himself. He even got as far as Britain but he did not leave a permanent base here. He even led his army as far as Egypt where he met Queen Cleopatra.

Eventually, he became dictator of Rome and wore the purple toga which the Emperors would later copy. But his fame made him a lot of enemies and he was stabbed to death in 44 BC.

This format could be applied to any number of historical figures:
• Florence Nightingale
• Henry VIII
• Martin Luther King

Toolbox for biography and autobiography

Start with a good opening line:

A cry rang out ...

This is the true, and remarkable, story of ...

X never wanted to be ordinary. He got his way.

X was a great leader.

Having established an eye-catching opening, use a roughly chronological framework: childhood, first steps to adulthood, adulthood, old age, death (as relevant).

Use an anecdote to point out a personal quality:

At six X developed a love of reading which would stay with him for life.

Let me take you back to a special day in my life.

Picture me at five.

Imagine me scoring the goal that won the Junior Trophy.

Use key words:
• crossroads
• turning point

Sum up with a telling last line:

Though X died young, she had already made a contribution which would secure her reputation.

In just a few years Y had made his mark. He would never be forgotten.

That early love of sport has stayed with me ever since, setting the tone for the coming years.

Maybe my love of art will lead to a career. I do hope so!

Lesson 12

Debates

Lesson Plan

Objective:	to write a debate, presenting opposite points of view.
Stimulus:	news reports, discussion of smoking.
Sentence level:	connectives, clear, coherent sentences.
Shared writing:	opening paragraph.
Guided writing:	debate on the rights and wrongs of smoking.

Structure of the lesson

Part 1

The teacher can give the pupils some extracts from the press on the debate over smoking in public. After a discussion of the main points the teacher should set out the structure of the debate:

• Introduction
• Arguments for
• Arguments against
• Re-state the key points. Put a personal opinion.

Part 2

The teacher could model the opening paragraph. In this introduction the writer should concisely establish why the debate matters, e.g. *A debate is raging: should smoking in public be banned?*

Part 3

In the first paragraph, set out the arguments put forward by opponents of smoking. What connectives will they use?

Firstly
Next
Also
Furthermore
What's more
More importantly

These phrases could be on a worksheet or a list on the board.

Part 4

In this paragraph, the pupils should put the counter arguments. It is not always easy for young children to be fair to a point of view with which they disagree. The teacher has to explain that they can put their own opinion in the conclusion but they have to present both sides fairly.

Some other connectives may come in here:
Now let's consider
In addition
Moreover
On the other hand

Part 5

In this concluding paragraph, the pupils should choose a key point which sums up the arguments of each side. Once this has been done, they can put their own point of view.

Some concluding connectives might be:
To sum up
On the one hand
On the other
Finally
To conclude
In summary
In conclusion

Examples of children's work

Should smoking in public be banned?

By Jennie Baker

Liverpool City Council plans to ban smoking in public. This decision has attracted a lot of debate in the city. Let's consider the arguments in favour and the arguments against.

This is what opponents of smoking say. Firstly, thousands of both young and elderly people die each year of heart disease and lung cancer. Some even die through passive smoking, breathing in other people's smoke. Millions of pounds is wasted on cigarettes that can sometimes kill you. Also, money is spent on patients in hospitals because of smoking and many families suffer because they have lost loved ones. Furthermore, there is the question of cleanliness. Many people, tourists and non-smokers alike, are disgusted and put off by the smell of nicotine, overflowing ashtrays, bad breath and yellow fingers. Cigarette stumps roll around the ground and stick to people's shoes. But, more importantly, they pollute the environment.

Now let's consider the arguments smokers put against this view. Smokers say it is a matter of choice. Why should anyone tell them what to do? It's a free country. In addition, smoking is very difficult and it is awfully hard to give up. Besides, it gives them lots of pleasure. Smoking helps them relax and calm down. Also, smokers add that there should be space for smokers and non-smokers in public areas and restaurants so that everyone has a choice. Moreover, in the opinion of smokers, it is only a minor issue. Why be so heavy-handed about it?

To sum up, on the one hand there is the argument about health and cleanliness. On the other, there is the argument about choice and freedom. Finally, to conclude, I personally think smoking should be banned. Smokers should be encouraged to stop. Then everyone could enjoy real freedom.

Comments

Jennie sets out her arguments clearly. There is a distinct four-paragraph structure. This organises the discussion. What's more, Jennie uses a wide range of varied connectives to order the discussion and keep it flowing. This is a measured, mature, well-argued piece of writing.

Suggestions

Other debates worth considering might be:
• Should boxing be banned?
• Which is better, football or cricket?
• Should the voting age be lowered?
• Is it right for advertisers to target children?

There are also debates about humanities topics:
• Did the Romans make Britain a better place?
• Was Henry VIII a good or bad king?
• What is good and bad about the local environment?

Toolbox

Use a four paragraph structure:
- Introduction – establish why the debate matters
- Arguments for
- Arguments against
- Conclusion- compare the main points of each sides argument and offer a personal opinion

Connectives are vital to the structure of a debate, providing a flow to the piece of writing:
- *firstly, secondly*
- *let's consider*
- *also*
- *furthermore*
- *what's more*
- *in addition*
- *moreover*
- *however*
- *Now let's consider*
- *On the one hand*
- *On the other*

Concluding connectives are equally important:
- *To sum up*
- *In conclusion*
- *In summary*
- *Finally*
- *Personally*
- *In my opinion*

Lesson 13

Interviews

Lesson Plan

Objective: to write about a historical or literary figure in the form of an interview.

Stimulus: a dramatised interview with Henry VIII.

Sentence level: questions and statements.

Shared writing: model a sample interview.

Guided writing: children write their own interview, with a historical or storybook character.

Interview with Henry VIII

INTERVIEWER: Your Majesty. Actually, that's a bit formal. Could I call you Henry?

HENRY VIII: Henry's fine.

INTERVIEWER: OK Hank, tell me about your early years.

HENRY VIII: I think we'll stick with Henry.

INTERVIEWER: Sorry. So Henry, how was your childhood and early manhood?

HENRY VIII: Oh, I had a privileged upbringing. I was sporty, popular with the ladies, good at my studies. Did you know I wrote a classic song?

INTERVIEWER: That would be 'Greensleeves', I assume?

HENRY VIII: Absolutely. Three and a half centuries and still going strong. They won't be saying that about Robbie Williams 350 years from now, will they? I was a terrific tennis player, if I say so myself. As for hunting, I was the business. There wasn't a boar or deer in southern England that felt safe from Henry the Hunt. (That was my nickname, you know).

INTERVIEWER: Quite. Now, you said you were a bit of a ladies' man. I suppose that explains the six wives.

HENRY VIII:	Mm, I did have a bit of a roving eye. There were a few disappointments though. I got a picture of one of my wives, Anne of Cleves, a real looker. But when she turned up at the door, the woman looked like a horse!
INTERVIEWER:	Of course, young Ann Boleyn lost her head over you.
HENRY VIII:	Who writes your jokes, Cranmer? That joke was old back in the sixteenth century.
INTERVIEWER:	Didn't you ever contemplate marriage guidance?
HENRY VIII:	Oh, I got plenty of that. Every courtier thought he was an expert on my love life.
INTERVIEWER:	But you did pretty much what you wanted?
HENRY VIII:	That's the point of being King.
INTERVIEWER:	You had a bit of a fall-out with the Catholic church, I hear.
HENRY VIII:	They stopped me getting a divorce! I mean, a King's supposed to get his own way, isn't he?
INTERVIEWER:	The monasteries had quite a bad time.
HENRY VIII:	Serves them right.
INTERVIEWER:	Finally, can I ask about your health?
HENRY VIII:	Ah, the gout. I'm afraid that was the result of too much rich food and fine wine. Still, life's there to be lived.
INTERVIEWER:	And you lived it to the full. Henry VIII, thank you, you're a star.
HENRY VIII:	I always was, my boy, I always was.

Structure of the lesson

Part 1

The teacher could use the above interview as an example or, in drama, get the children to break into groups and brainstorm questions and answers for a famous celebrity, sporting figure, historical or story book figure. The youngsters could even put on a drama, interviewing their chosen character. From this brainstorming session, the teacher could get them to comment on the questions and answers which worked well.

While exploring the word play that goes into doing a good interview, she could point out the conventions. An interview breaks into an alternating pattern:

1 Interviewer poses a question. Remember your question mark.
2 Interviewee answers. This time it is a statement. Full stop.

In the course of the lesson it may be suitable to point out the opportunities to include exclamations and exclamation marks.

Part 2

Once brainstorming has taken place and the teacher has identified the conventions of an interview, the teacher can give the children some sample questions and ask them to come up with answers. They may be provided with a prompt sheet or notes they have taken themselves to aid their memory. A good idea is to ask them to answer two or three questions to begin with and talk them through. She could then read out some good examples.

Part 3

The class can now conclude the interview with a further two or three questions. The more able pupils might want to invent some extra questions and answers of their own. As usual, the teacher should stress to her pupils that the final question and answer should be among the strongest, to end the piece of writing on a high note.

Examples of children's work

Interview with the Big Bad Wolf

By Megan Harding, Year 6

Interviewer: What was your childhood like?

Big Bad Wolf: I was a cute and happy cub. I went to Blewdown Primary School.

Interviewer: What was your favourite subject in school?

Big Bad Wolf: Choir. I could howl a good tune. Oh, and dinner time. I liked pork the best.

Interviewer: Did you have any problems?

Big Bad Wolf: I didn't like the little girl in red across the road.

Interviewer: What was your first job?

Big Bad Wolf: I was a butcher.

Interviewer: What are your hopes for the future?

Big Bad Wolf: That's easy, I've got to get rid of those three little pigs!

Interview with Julius Caesar

Group work, Yorkshire

Interviewers: When did you know that you had a talent for warfare?

Caesar: Oh, that was very early on. I was kidnapped by pirates but I went back and taught them a lesson they won't forget.

Interviewers: Didn't you kill them?

Caesar: Well, they won't do it again, will they?

Interviewers: Then you fell in love with Cleopatra, didn't you?

Caesar: Yes, she was beautiful. Ah, Cleo.

Interviewers: Anyway, you went back to warfare, didn't you?

Caesar: I did. I outdid all my competitors and earned the finest reputation in the Republic. I conquered the Gauls. The Battle of Alesia was a triumph.

Interviewers: Didn't you have a tough time with Vercingetorix though?

Caesar: I beat him, didn't I?

Interviewers: You killed him too.

Caesar: Dead men don't fight back!

Interviewers: You're quite ruthless, aren't you?

Caesar: Very.

Interviewers: So why didn't you stop Brutus and the others?

Caesar: Er ....

<u>Interviewers:</u>   You got a letter, after all.

<u>Caesar:</u>   Oh yes, that letter. We all make mistakes.

<u>Interviewers:</u>   How was Britain?

<u>Caesar:</u>   Wet and not a bit friendly. I didn't stay long.

<u>Interviewers:</u>   Looking back, is there anything you would change?

<u>Caesar:</u>   Yes, I'd take more notice of that letter about the Ides of March!

Comments

Megan uses the format very confidently. She gets the humour by remaining in character throughout the interview. One particularly striking answer is when the Big Bad Wolf says he doesn't like the little girl in red across the road. Here, she is using the techniques of tension used in fiction lessons. Saying 'little girl in red' rather than 'Little Red Riding Hood' achieves a comic effect by playing a kind of guessing game with the reader. She also demonstrates the use of exclamation marks, full stops and question marks in context. This can be reinforced by getting the pupils to read their work exaggerating the effect of the punctuation to reinforce its use in conveying meaning.

The Julius Caesar interview is very sophisticated and witty. The group had a couple of very articulate children and the contributions of all five dovetailed successfully to create a very polished overall effect. Sometimes children who are quite articulate but have problems with recording (dyslectic perhaps) can excel in group work like this.

Extensions might be interviews with:
• a Yanomami Indian
• a child from another country
• a child in the Blitz
• Boudicca
• a Suffragette
• a religious figure

Toolbox

An interview follows an alternating pattern.
Interviewer:
Interviewee:

The interviewer asks questions. Punctuate with a question mark.

The interviewee answers with a statement. Punctuate with a full stop.

Occasionally, the interviewer might also use a statement, e.g.
Tell me about your childhood.

An interview often asks questions in chronological order. The pattern is sometimes broken when the interviewer prioritises the opening and closing question or pursues a particular area of the interviewee's life.

Lesson 14

Letters

Lesson Plan

Objective: to write a letter.

Stimulus: *The Jolly Postman* by Allan and Janet Ahlberg; and the letter from Hengist to Horsa (opposite).

Sentence level: coherent sentences.

Shared writing: model a letter.

Guided writing: children write a letter applying to be a replacement for Harry Potter.

Structure of the lesson

Part 1

The teacher could model a letter by a fictional character (there is a sample below). She could then discuss with her pupils the basic features of the letter:
- address and date in the top right-hand corner
- below the address and date and on the left you have your greeting: *Dear Sir/Dear Madam*, etc.
- start your letter on the next line, indenting the first line. This should be a brief explanation of the reason for the letter.
- the next paragraph outlines the basic argument or information contained in the letter.
- the final paragraph summarises the key points in the letter and thanks the reader for taking the time to read the letter.
- the writer closes back on the right hand side with *Yours faithfully, Yours sincerely,* etc.

Part 2

Having reminded the pupils of the basic structure of a letter, the teacher should then introduce each section in bite-sized pieces, setting the scene and reminding the youngsters of basic points each time. In this section the teacher could ask the children to write the address, date and greeting, establishing where they go.

In the Harry Potter letter, an address in Privet Drive makes sense, near Harry's. The greeting should be the Minister of Witchcraft.

Part 3

In this short section, a paragraph in its own right, ask the pupils to explain to the reader why the letter is being sent. The Harry Potter letter takes the form of a job application for the vacant post of wizard.

Part 4

This contains the main argument of the letter. Here, the pupils give their qualifications and life experience for being a wizard.

Part 5

Here the children close by thanking the reader and bidding farewell in the time-honoured fashion: *Yours ...*

A model letter to act as a stimulus for the class:

A letter from Hengist to Horsa, in the year 450

Fourth cottage on the left,
The Hamlet,
East Anglia,
British Isles.
July 1st, 450.

Dear Horsa,

I hope all is well with you, dear brother. Just a brief line to let you know how the scouting trip to the British Isles is going.

The day we've been waiting for has arrived! Yes, the Romans are leaving. With their Empire crumbling, our Latin friends are upping sticks and heading back to the Eternal City. This is a terrific opportunity. Can you rustle up some of our hardy Anglo-Saxon warriors and pop across the North Sea? After years of Roman occupation, the Celts have grown soft. They're in no condition to resist. Britain is rich with wheat, tin, livestock and iron. Don't delay. Get the fleet ready now! We can make this island ours.

That's all for now. Say hello to the family and I hope to see you and your warriors soon.

Brotherly greetings,

Yours faithfully,

Hengist.

Examples of children's work

16, Privet Drive,
Prescot,
Merseyside,
L34 2TA.

Dear Minister of Witchcraft,

I am writing to you to apply for the post of wizard. I have always been interested in the Dark Arts.

I have the following GCSE qualifications:
- Levitation for the advanced
- Transfiguration 1, 2 and 3
- Muggle Studies
- Daring spells
- Divination
- Defence in Quidditch

I also have experience of the following. I have soared the heavens on my Nimbus 2002. I have turned my teacher into a Slytherin mascot.
I have even wrestled with the Great Fluffy.

I am looking forward to hearing from you soon. Thank you for reading my letter.
Yours faithfully,
Heather Davies.

A letter to an arsonist

By Matthew Garrett

(N.B. Matthew's school was burned down by arsonists. This letter was part of the campaign to re-build the school community).

Simonswood Primary School,
Westhead Avenue,
Kirkby,
Merseyside.
May 7th, 2002.

Dear Fire-raiser,

I am writing to you to ask why you started the fire.

Do you know what damage you caused? You have wasted the firemen's time. Teachers and children have had to move school and, as if that isn't enough, the mayhem you caused has ruined all our work.

The thing I don't understand is why you did it. Were you bored? Did you get peer pressure? Were you showing off? Did you want to make kids upset?

Since the fire we have been building a new Simonswood. I think you should do something with your life. You could confess then help out some kids. Doing a lecture on how crime doesn't pay might be a good idea.

Yours angrily,

Matthew Garrett.

Comments

Heather's letter follows the conventions. All the sentences are coherent and the voice is consistent throughout. She also uses bullet points to make a list. She exhibits an engaging sense of humour. Altogether, this is a very confident piece of work.

Matthew's very intelligent response to a serious event in the life of the school is well-structured and extremely articulately argued. This work helped the school community heal after a terrible shock and was featured on local radio.

Suggestions

Similar activities could include:
- a letter from an alien reporting home about planet Earth (see the Dr Xargle books by Jean Willis).
- a letter home from a Roman soldier on Hadrian's Wall (see Roman Wall Blues by W.H.Auden re-printed in Teach Me to Write Poetry by Alan Gibbons).
- a letter from the Big Bad Wolf apologising to either Little Red Riding Hood or the Three Pigs.
- a letter arguing for the repair of the local playground.

Toolbox

Put the address and date in the top right-hand corner.

Write the greeting *Dear ...* in the left-hand side. Make sure it goes below the address and date but on the opposite side of the page.

On the line below the greeting, indent the first line. Here, give the reason for the letter.

Start a new paragraph. Put the main argument of the letter. Make it clear. The sentences should be simple and direct.

Start a new paragraph. Thank your reader for taking the time to read the letter.

On the right-hand side, close with *Yours faithfully* or *Yours sincerely*.

Consider connectives:
- *Firstly, secondly*
- *Furthermore*
- *Also*
- *What's more*
- *However*
- *So*
- *Even*
- *That said,*
- *In conclusion*
- *To conclude*
- *Finally*

Lesson 15

Postcards

Lesson Plan

> *Objective:* to write a postcard.
>
> *Stimulus:* a selection of holiday postcards.
>
> *Sentence level:* simple sentences, capital letters, full stops.
>
> *Shared writing:* modelling a short holiday postcard.
>
> *Guided writing:* children write their own postcards, based on storybook or historical figures.

Structure of the lesson

Part 1

The teacher allows the children to browse a selection of picture postcards and collect phrases that crop up more than once. They should make a list for discussion. On the basis of the discussion, the teacher can use a photocopiable template on OHP and demonstrate a short holiday postcard, highlighting the various features.

Part 2

The teacher can now set the children off to work on their own picture postcards related to a story they have read, or to a history, geography, RE or PSHE topic they have been studying.

She should demonstrate that the first sentence is a general one, saying hello or outlining the purpose of the postcard.

Part 2

She can now ask the children to write the main part of the postcard, describing the holiday destination or other main information. What kind of sentences will they use given the restricted space available? Stress short statements.

Part 3

Close with a greeting, not usually as formal as in a letter.

If there is time, the children can describe a stamp and draw a picture on the other side of the postcard, making it a picture postcard.

Postcard from Gretel

Wood cutter's cottage,
Dark woods,
Stonyville
LA5 6JJ

Dear dad,

Just a line to let you know we are both ok.

Don't feel too bad about leaving us in the woods. We know that our wicked step mother made you.

Our new landlady is weird. She also lives in a house made of sweets. Guess what? she's only trying to fatten up Hansel! I wonder why.

Anyway, we're trying to make the best of a bad job.

We both hope to see you soon.

Love
Gretel.

Postcard from a Roman soldier on Hadrian's Wall

CIVIS ROMANUS SUM

10 DENARI

Dear Varinia,

Just a line to say hello. How are you and the kids?

It's wet and cold here on the Wall. Caledonia can be pretty miserable in winter. That reminds me, I could do with a few pairs of woolly socks. The Picts have been causing a bit of trouble but nothing we can't handle. I am a bit homesick though still eight more years and my tour of duty is over.

Please write back and don't forget the socks.

love

Marcus
x x x

Villa VII

Via Sorrento

Pompeii

Italia

Examples of children's work

Comments

The first postcard develops the Hansel and Gretel story, outlining the story in a shorter format. It uses a variety of punctuation and will supplement fiction-writing as an approach to exploring the narrative. The postcard from the Roman soldier demonstrates how cross-curricular work can be imaginative and interesting. It offers opportunities for design and illustration and there is a good product to display.

Other examples might be:
• an apology from the Big Bad Wolf to the Three Little Pigs or Little Red Riding Hood
• an alien writes home while on holiday on Planet Earth

Other subjects in the curriculum can also be enlivened using postcards e.g.:
• a Viking sends a postcard from Lindisfarne
• Vasco da Gama sends a postcard from India

Suggestions

The children could write emails. This is especially good in an IT lesson when they can see the format on the screen.
What do email addresses look like? What elements do they have to have?

Do writers express themselves as formally in emails?

Toolbox

A postcard has two elements:
• The address of the person you are writing to.
• A short, usually quite informal message. (Sentences should be short and snappy. There is limited space.)

Postcards usually tell people how a holiday is going, so the first sentence might sum up how it is going.

The second sentence might list some of the things the writer has been doing.

Finally, you should sum up the whole experience and perhaps express a wish to see the correspondent soon.

The farewell will probably be more informal than in a letter.

So *Yours* or *See you soon*.

Lesson 16

School reports

Lesson Plan

Objective: to write a report.

Stimulus: a school report (see example overleaf).

Sentence level: a range of punctuation.

Shared writing: modelling a report card.

Guided writing: children write a school report for a historical or story book character.

Structure of the lesson

Part 1

In this section the teacher could model her own sample report card or use the sample below. She could then demonstrate the kind of phrases a teacher might use in this kind of writing. She could also demonstrate the punctuation used in:

- sentences
- questions
- exclamations

Part 2

Having modelled a sample report the teacher could ask the children to fill in two subjects of the report at a time, going over some of the conventions and sharing good examples with the pupils.

Part 3

Now complete the final two or three subjects, following the same model. Ask the children to go over the whole exercise, reading the sentences in their heads and checking that the sentences are properly punctuated. The context gives them a clue. Another strategy is to read one or two out loud, exaggerating them to identify the punctuation.

A school report
Count Dracula

Name: Count Dracula aka Count Alucard.

Date: June 1st, 2005.

Intelligence

Supernaturally high. Wily, cunning and utterly malevolent. The young Count is easily the brightest boy in class. Unfortunately, he uses his considerable IQ to wreak havoc around the school. Definitely on the road to ruin.

Appearance

The whole staff are extremely worried about Dracula's ghastly pallor, piercing red eyes and dreadful teeth. I suggest you take him to an anaemia clinic and an orthodontist – immediately!

P.E.

Though a rather sickly looking child, Dracula excels at flying. To be honest, he drives us quite batty by flitting round the gymnasium.

Subjects

Dracula's best subject is Maths. Boy, can he count! He also enjoys Biology but the other children are getting bored of studying the circulatory system every lesson – all that blood!

Manners

This is not really Dracula's strongpoint. Does he have to hypnotise everyone and drain their blood? It really is most tiresome.

Head teacher's comments

Dracula has had a difficult year. By the way, has he mentioned anything about Mr Van Helsing? Our Deputy Head Teacher has been missing for six months. We are gravely concerned.

Examples of children's work

School report

Donald Duck

By Kirsty Roscoe, Year 6

Intelligence

None. I would recommend a special talking school. Donald has no intelligence, just the intelligence to shout out quack. He goes nuts when he sees a chipmunk. Quack!! He has gone quackers!!

Appearance

Needs to remove the sailor's hat in class and quack-cellent at shining his beak. An ultra shine! He appears to have no shoes. I think he should get some wide enough for his webbed feet and get some pants!

PE

Awful at swimming. He is a duck! Don't you think he should be able to swim? We are giving him a special swimming lesson. One time, Lisa was drowning. Donald tried to save her and nearly drowned himself!

Subjects

Great at Duck language. We went on a school trip and all the ducks tried to snatch our sandwiches. Donald saved us, saying, 'Go away!' But he did give them his sandwiches. He is such a sweet duck.

Manners

Awful! Absolutely awful. When he sees a sweet, little chipmunk, he goes NUTS! He scares the chipmunk away. He stays like that for half an hour. He needs to learn a lot of manners if he is to make progress.

Comments

Kirsty uses the full range of punctuation. She adopts a teacherly voice in an engaging manner to comic effect.

Suggestions

Other activities might be school reports for:
- Boudicca
- Queen Victoria
- Roald Dahl
- Shakespeare

Toolbox

School reports have a certain sort of language. Teachers express themselves in a way that tells parents what they mean without being too direct.

Hold a class discussion of these phrases.

Make a template of the various categories about which the children will write:
- Appearance
- Behaviour
- Subjects
- Intelligence
- PE
- Manners

Demonstrate how punctuation is used in context:
- Statements using full stops
- Questions using question marks
- Exclamations when you stress points, raise a voice, etc., using exclamation marks
- Clauses or lists, using commas

Demonstrate how humour is delivered by referring to a character's personality indirectly or through word play, e.g. 'Donald is quackers!'

Lesson 17

Character sketches

Lesson Plan

Objective: to write a character sketch.

Stimulus: discussion of storybook characters, and 'Darth Vader' character sketch.

Sentence level: a range of punctuation.

Shared writing: demonstrate a character sketch.

Guided writing: children write their own sketch of Harry Potter.

A character sketch: Darth Vader

He's a dark lord whose shadow falls across the known universe. He is cinema's most famous heavy-breather. Striking terror into the hearts of rebel fighters everywhere, this steel-helmeted fallen Jedi is one of the great movie villains.

Starting out as a talented young Jedi, Darth Vader is a man seduced by the dark side. Picture him striding through the labyrinth of corridors in the Death Star, gloved hand ready to pull his light sabre. Though devoted to the evil Emperor, Vader has an Achilles' heel. One day he will allow his feelings for his long-lost son Luke Skywalker to break through, a moment of humanity which will lead to his destruction.

If you are wondering how to spot Darth Vader in a crowd, wonder no more. Can you imagine a cross between a robot and a vampire? Well, that's Vader! Look out for these features: steel helmet (black), long cloak (also black), boots (yes, you've got it, black again). With his trademark heavy breathing, Darth Vader would stand out even in the most crowded street.

Darth Vader is the heir to a long tradition of great villains. He is one of Hollywood's greatest blockbuster bad guys. He lives at the heart of darkness. His is a story of betrayal, cruelty and redemption. It is the stuff of nightmares, and of legends.

Structure of the lesson

Part 1

The teacher should read through the modelled character sketch and point out the features which make it readable and eye-catching. The sketch uses the techniques of tension, picking out some general statements about the character without giving away who it is. This acts as a general introduction. The second paragraph outlines the character's personality. The third describes his appearance while the fourth summarises his impact. She can point out the various conventions.

Part 2

Now it is the children's turn. Three or four outlining general comments about the unnamed character catch the reader's attention.

Part 3

This paragraph is about the character's personality. The teacher can model subordinate clauses such as this: *'Starting out as a talented young Jedi, Darth Vader is a man seduced by the dark side.'*

Questions and exclamations help give some texture to the writing. Addressing the reader with phrases such as: *Imagine him ...* or *Picture him ...* will help too.

Part 4

This paragraph outlines the character's appearance. It is better to delay this paragraph. Youngsters often think this is all they have to write. The teacher could suggest suitable connectives the youngsters might use. Note: connectives have to be relevant. There has been a tendency to pepper writing with them!

Part 5

Finally, the teacher should discuss a generalised conclusion. A useful trick here is to make a list of what his story is about. Use a colon and commas.

Examples of children's work

Character sketch: Harry Potter

By Amanda (Roby Park Primary School, Year 6)

He is a boy wizard. He fights evil. He is the main character in best-selling books by J.K.Rowling. He is also the star of the Hollywood blockbuster films.

Brought up in the county of Surrey, he is an orphan. He attends Hogwarts school. During his time there he has made friends with Ron Weasely and Hermione Granger. He is the star of the Quidditch team. While he is learning to use his magic, he likes to have adventures. His arch-enemies are Draco Malfoy, Crabbe and Goyle. One character, above all, haunts the books – Voldemort!

But how would you recognise Harry? Look for the thunderbolt and lightning scar, big, round glasses and untidy hair. With his trademark black cloak and uniform with a Griffindor crest, he is unmissable.

Harry's story is one of: magic, good, evil and courage. He is a hero for today.

Character sketch: Count Dracula

By Karl (Roby Park)

He is very evil. He is best known as the Prince of Darkness. He is one of the scariest characters in books and films. You wouldn't want his hand on your shoulder!

Count Dracula lives in an old castle in Transylvania. He has the ability to fly. Perhaps you might even see him turn into a bat. His fangs are big and pointy and he has a very pale face. He preys on young girls to drink their blood. You would see his blazing eyes from many yards away. His long, black cloak could scare you witless. They even say he lives forever.

Dracula has jet black hair and a pale face. He has long, pointy claws. Beware, they're as sharp as a razor blade. He hisses when he pronounces his words. His back-combed black hair is as black as coal, and very greasy. He rests in a coffin. Note, his reflection can't be seen in a mirror.

So that's Count Dracula. His story is all about horror, fear and evil. Don't have nightmares!

Character sketch: Henry VIII

By Ryan (Huyton with Roby CE School, Year 6)

He is one of the most famous kings of England. Cruel and ruthless, he has a gruesome reputation. Although he is not too popular with women, he is known all around the world and children still study him today.

But what kind of man was he? Sport was one of his greatest loves. His personal favourites were: archery, hunting, tennis and jousting. He also had an interest in music so he wrote his own song called Greensleeves.

However, he did have a love of food, so his sporting days stopped when he started to get too fat! His dancing days also came to an end. He had a disease called gout and ulcers on his legs. He would, of course, upset Jamie Oliver with his dislike of healthy food!

Above all, two things make him memorable. The first was that he had six wives, two of whom were beheaded. His favourite wife, Jane Seymour, died naturally. One survived and he divorced the other two. He would have had to abdicate but another major thing that he did was to create his own church, the Church of England. That way he could make his own rules. All in all, he had quite a career!

So how would you spot him in a crowd? Look out for an awfully fat person and note his big, smelly, gouty foot. Also, you will see his magnificent golden crown and his posh clothes.

To sum up, when you think of Henry VIII you will see: obesity, ugliness and a cruel and ruthless beheader!

Comments

Amanda's character sketch is fluently written. It observes clear conventions. It employs a wide range of punctuation and also uses connectives to help it flow. In his sketch of Dracula, Karl structures his writing well, opening with general statements about the character. He uses good imperative verbs such as *Note*, and sums up well with the phrase *So that's Count Dracula* and the exhortation not to have nightmares. Ryan's sketch of Henry VIII is confident in its use of subordinate clauses and connectives such as *although*, *however* and *above all*. There is a good pace and structure to the piece and he has an eye-catching final paragraph.

Toolbox

A character sketch is about the personality, reputation and appearance of the figure considered.

A good structure might be:
• An introduction outlining the character's general reputation
• A paragraph about his/her personality
• A paragraph about his/her appearance
• A conclusion which summarises his/her importance

Vary your sentences: statements, exclamations and questions.

Consider your connectives such as: *also, even, what's more, however*.

You might list the character's qualities. Don't forget to use commas.

Don't forget connectives such as *finally, to conclude, to sum up* as you complete the conclusion.

Lesson 18

Invitations

Lesson Plan

Objective: to write an invitation.

Stimulus: a sample invitation, either kept from a party or engagement or modelled by the teacher.

Sentence level: short sentences, note forms.

Shared writing: teacher models an example with suggestions by the pupils.

Guided writing: pupils write their own invitation to a Halloween party.

Structure of the lesson

Part 1

The teacher hands out photocopies of some sample invitations and draws attention to the various features. The invitation should contain the following:
- name of the event
- where it is held
- what day it is held
- what time it is held
- what kind of event it is
- what the guest should wear or bring with them

It can be decorated appropriately with illustrations or highlighted features.

Part 2

A useful strategy, particularly for young children, is for the teacher to write the requirements on a whiteboard and ask them to do two at a time, rubbing out the guides as she goes. Start with an overall title for the event and what day it takes place.

Part 3

Now ask the children to give the time it begins and ends, what will be going on and where to reply. Explain the phrase RSVP. Even the youngest children enjoy playing with terms like this, especially if you ham up the French. There is a tendency among some adults to talk down to children. Maybe that explains the bizarre voice some people adopt when addressing the early years. Put across information in a pacey, fun way and it is surprising what they can absorb and retain. Playing with language is a key learning strategy.

Part 4

Now the children can illustrate the invitation. This shouldn't just be pretty pictures. The teacher can demonstrate speech bubbles, thought bubbles and other ways to present snippets of information. Every culture has combined text and illustration. A classroom that doesn't is in danger of dying of boredom!

Examples of children's work

An invitation to the Big Bad Wolf's birthday party

By John K, Year 3

You are invited to my birthday party.
When: the next full moon.
Where: Wolf cottage, Dark Woods Lane.
What time: sunset till late. (Little pigs shouldn't worry about the time.
They won't be going home!)

There will be lots to do:
* dancing
* dressing up as grannies
* pass the parcel
* howling at the moon

RSVP:
B.B.Wolf,
Wolf Cottage,
Dark Woods Lane.
BB1 2WW.
Email: wolf@huffnpuff.co.uk

An invitation to a Halloween party
By Michael F., Year 1

Comments

John's invitation includes all the necessary information. There are lots of humorous touches and a there is very clever email address at the end.

Michael observes the conventions and produces a lively, animated invitation. The essential information is well set out and readable. *The Jolly Postman* by Allan and Janet Ahlberg is another important resource in encouraging the children to write invitations.

Suggestions

Other ideas might be:
• an invitation to Harry Potter's graduation from Hogwarts
• an invitation to Henry VIII's latest wedding
• an invitation by a Celtic chief to Julius Caesar to visit Britain

Toolbox

Presentation: put the invitation in a border so you can decorate it later with speech bubbles, cartoons, etc.

Give the invitation a title to catch the reader's, attention e.g.:
It's my birthday!
Jenny Wilson is fifteen!
Come to my party!

The teacher can list the information the youngsters need to provide on the blackboard and go through them systematically during the lesson:
Who is holding the event?
When is it?
What time?
Where?
Do you have to bring anything?
What will the guests be doing/eating?

Close with an RSVP (Répondez, s'il vous plait) – 'reply please' in French).

Include an address, phone number and email. Demonstrate how to set them out.

Lesson 19

Posters

Lesson Plan

Objective: to design a poster.

Stimulus: posters collected by the teacher (movie posters, restaurant promotions, etc).

Sentence level: short, coherent sentences and questions.

Shared writing: teacher demonstrates how to construct text boxes and combine text and illustration.

Guided writing: children design Comic Relief posters.

Structure of the lesson

Part 1

The teacher should point out the main features of posters. The key here is to demonstrate that the children should combine text and illustration. A poster isn't a pretty picture with a title. She can demonstrate how to highlight different pieces of text using borders and different colours. Turning to the children's own task, she can highlight the various sections or boxes:

- a heading – the reader has to know it is Comic Relief!
- where the contributor's money will be going
- why it is useful
- persuasive writing – how a little can go a long way
- the conditions of the people to whom the donations are going
- fun activities to raise the money
- good slogans that will stay in the reader's mind

Part 2

Now it is the children's turn. As ever, it is good to break the lesson into bite-sized pieces. Without some kind of structure, many children will produce a product which is poorly organised and presented. Start perhaps with the title and a slogan. Then move on to one box, summing up where the donor's money is going.

Part 3

After looking at some examples, the teacher can now ask the children to work on the boxes, explaining what money has provided in the past and why it is needed. What are conditions in the relief areas like?

Part 4

Finally, the children could include other features. In this case, what fund-raising activities are happening locally? These could go in a separate box on the poster. Then they can illustrate the rest of the poster with cut-out photos or hand-drawn pictures of their own. It helps if they are bold, simple and emblematic. Complicated drawings are less likely to catch the attention of the reader.

Poster for a Dracula movie

By children at St Joseph's Primary School

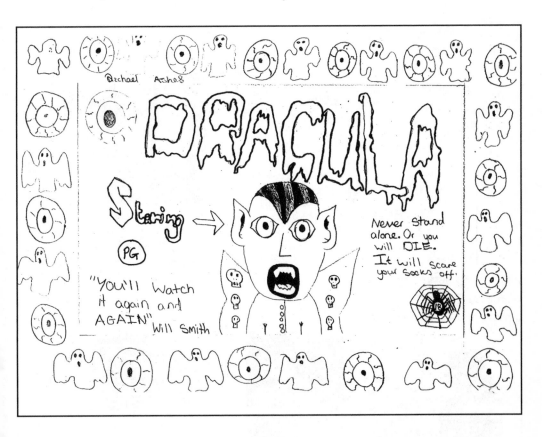

Posters for Comic Relief

Group work at Roby Park Primary School

It's all about you helping!

Every Penny helps

Where your money goes!
Only 26p can feed a child for a day and £100 can build a shelter. £10 can give a child a life by giving them an immunizatino matter how small, it all adds up.

What you can do with your money!

When you buy a red nose or biscuit your money will go to people in different countries.

PLEASE give generously

Contact
Tel: 0151 480 921
fax: 0151 802 509
email: Comic Relief@home.com

By giving your money you could make the world a better place for poorer people.

These three children need your help so please donate some money PLEASE!!!

COMIC RELIEF

Just do something!

This is what some of your money can do

£100 - can build a shelter home

26p - can feed a person for a day (it can feed people!)

£10 - enough for a medicine kit

£3 - Will help a water supply running

Every little helps

Your money can help in many different countrys and ways.

Last comic relief £300 helped build a clinic. No-one could of done it with the money of your help.

Can you find a place in your heart to give as little as 1p? No matter how small it is remember IT ALL AD'S up!

These children need food and your money can help

Ten years ago a terrible flood came and destroyed many homes. Your money can help rebuild after that terrible disaster.

you can buy a biscuit for 10p in school. you can also wear red clothes and hair.

Rember Just do something !

Comments

The posters are eye catching and convey the essential information. The different areas of the poster are clearly marked out. The title, illustrations and text all complement each other. The odd error of grammar or syntax could be pointed out later e.g. *could of* instead of *could have*. These minor errors hardly detract from the success of these pieces of work.

Another activity children enjoy is designing a movie poster to accompany a story they have been reading.

Suggestions

Here are some more ideas:
- a safety poster
- school rules
- the all-new Ten Commandments
- posters for a school play
- posters for a Keep Our School Tidy campaign

Toolbox

Presentation is important in a poster.

There should be:
- a large, bold, simple, eye-catching slogan
- a good, simple illustration
- text giving information (separate boxes, bullet-pointing, colour-coded writing, etc. all help to deliver the essential facts and information to the reader). N.B.: the most important reason that posters don't work is that the youngsters think they are just a pretty picture. It is the delivery of simple pieces of text which makes them successful.
- the name of the designer/publisher, perhaps with an email address

If it is a film poster it should have:
- title
- film-maker
- actors
- a good illustration from the movie

- a certificate
- a blurb or catchphrase – *In space nobody can hear you scream.*
- a quote from a newspaper/magazine – *'A must-see movie', Yorkshire Post.*
- a phrase such as *Showing at good cinemas everywhere.*

Lesson 20

Writing a report

> ## Lesson Plan
>
> *Objective:* to write a report.
>
> *Stimulus:* a school trip.
>
> *Sentence level:* variety of punctuation.
>
> *Shared writing:* an opening paragraph.
>
> *Guided writing:* children use the example of the modelled paragraph to write their own reports.

Structure of the lesson

Part 1

Children get used to the idea that, after going on a school trip, they have to write about it. Much of this writing is routine and unsatisfying. One reason for this is that children don't reflect on the visit but just mention a few details. The teacher should demonstrate how they can enliven their writing following this plan:

Paragraph 1: anticipation. What did they expect from the trip?

Paragraph 2: what they did before lunch and how they felt about it.

Paragraph 3: lunch and the afternoon. Again, how they felt about the activity brings the report to life.

Paragraph 4: the trip home and getting back to school. Reflecting on the experience.

She could then model a paragraph, based on the children's ideas, describing the sense of expectation before the visit.

Part 2

In this paragraph the children should include arriving at the destination, what people said, what there was to see and do. Anecdotes bring a report to life.

Part 3

This paragraph describes lunch and everything that happened in the afternoon session. The teacher could demonstrate a variety of punctuation in context, e.g. *What did I find? It was seaweed.*

Part 4

Finally, the pupils talk about the trip home and how they felt after getting back to school. What was their favourite part of the day?

Examples of children's work

School trip to Freshfield

By Liam, Year 3

I didn't know what to expect from our school trip. Mr Gibbons said there were rare red squirrels and we would be able to go for a walk along the beach. It didn't sound very exciting but I was wrong!

It was a short coach trip so I didn't feel sick. Mr Gibbons had to tell some of the children not to start eating their packed lunches! When we got there we bought packets of nuts to feed to the squirrels. There was a path through the forest and we couldn't see much at first. Suddenly I saw one of the red squirrels. They are smaller and cuter than the grey ones, with pointed ears. Then we went for a run down the hills. Mr Gibbons yelled: 'Geronimo!' Mrs Horabin gave him a funny look.

We had our packed lunch on the wooden tables but wasps kept buzzing round. They were a pain. They made kids squeal. After lunch we went down to the beach. The rangers helped us fill in worksheets about the shells we found. Guess what I found? There were razor shells. Here are some of the things we noticed: shells, seaweed, driftwood and a lot of rubbish.

Some kids fell asleep on the bus home but I didn't. I joined in the singing which got louder and louder. When we got home I was glad to see my dad. I'd had a great day.

Comments

Liam's report is well-structured. There is a build-up. Events are related systematically. He uses clear, coherent sentences. Exclamation marks and question marks are employed to vary the text. There is also a good conclusion.

Liam's report works because it follows the pattern of breaking it into bite-sized pieces:
- anticipation – what did he expect
- the journey there
- the main attractions of the day
- lunch
- the journey home and reflections on the day

Suggestions

Some other ideas might be:
- a visitor to school
- a big sporting event
- a visit to see a much-hyped movie
- a birthday party

Toolbox

To get the best out of a report, discuss these elements:

Firstly, anticipation: what were the participants' expectations of the day?

Secondly, the journey there: can the writers find some interesting anecdotes about the teachers and children?

Thirdly (and this is the part most children include in routine reports): tell the reader what happened when they got there.

To conclude: describe the aftermath.

This structure is far more satisfying than a simple list of what happened.

Lesson 21

Presenting information
A natural history

Lesson Plan

Objective: to present information.

Stimulus: books and magazines about a particular animal, for example a lion. (This works well after a visit to the zoo).

Sentence level: coherent sentences.

Shared writing: modelling a sample natural history.

Guided writing: children write the natural history of a mythological creature e.g. a dragon.

Structure of the lesson

Part 1

In groups, the children browse information material about the lion. The teacher uses the information they have collected to model a sample piece of information writing. She demonstrates how to order the bare facts into something that is ordered and coherent, using headings and sub-headings and a range of punctuation.

She can then send the children off with some new information books or fact sheets. This material they are going to order into a short natural history, either of another animal or of a fictitious or mythological creature.

Part 2

The children write the headline (the creature's name) and, in parentheses, give it a fake Latin name.

They then write the sub-heading: *Habitat.*

This first section details the creature's habitat. The teacher should explain that this means where it lives, not just the area but the kind of home it makes for itself. She can demonstrate the various sentence structures they can use to deliver information:
• simple and complex sentences
• questions

- lists
- exclamations
- parentheses

Part 3

The children write the sub-heading: *Appearance*.

Using the same variety of sentence structures, the teacher asks the pupils to describe the creature's appearance. A good idea would be to make a list in one paragraph, using commas and another in the next paragraph, using bullet points.

Part 4

The children write the sub-heading: *Behaviour*.

This final paragraph deals with the creature's behaviour. Is it fierce? What does it eat? She should remind them to tie everything up with an effective final sentence.

Examples of children's work

Natural history of the dragon (Draco Draconus)

By Thomas S, Year 6

Habitat
Being a solitary creature, the dragon prefers lonely, deserted places such as mountain tops and hidden caves. The dragon's ability to fly means that it can nest on even the most inaccessible peaks and summits. It can also be found in dark forests and gloomy swamps.

Appearance
The dragon is easy to spot. It has a huge wingspan and can fly at tremendous speed. It can even breathe fire from its nostrils. Note also the following features:
- metallic scales
- long, pointed tail
- razor-sharp claws
- curved, flesh-ripping fangs

Dragons come in many different colours: green, red and gold. It doesn't come in pink!

Behaviour
The dragon is a ferocious beast. It preys on small villages and is carnivorous. It has a particular liking for young maidens. Though it usually likes fresh meat, it has been known to enjoy canned food such as knights in shining armour. Though it can live for thousands of years, the dragon finds modern life tough. Few are seen, so few they are rumoured to be extinct. Well, have you seen one lately?

Comments

Thomas' work is well-organised and uses clear sub-headings to demarcate the three sections. Lists are written using both commas and bullet points. He uses questions and exclamations to vary the text. This is a successful piece of information writing.

The children could write about any mythological creature from their reading:
• the Minotaur
• a vampire
• a werewolf

They could even describe their teacher as a mythological creature!

Natural history of Mr Harris
(Harris Horrendous)

Habitat
A solitary creature by nature, the English teacher inhabits the front of the classroom, vainly trying to introduce thirty children to the delights of syntax, grammar and punctuation, poetry and literature. He is also often seen foraging in stockrooms looking at books. This behaviour is known as browsing. It is rumoured that the English teacher has a home but he is rarely seen out of school.

Appearance
Often distinguished by his tweed jacket and elbow pads, the English teacher usually wears glasses, the product of constant reading. His shoulders are bowed from marking. He is sometimes twitchy due to continual coffee drinking.

Behaviour

The English teacher spends many hours teaching and marking. Curiously, though this behaviour is common, it doesn't seem to give the English teacher much pleasure. He engages in a constant growl, known as English teacher's grumble. This growl rises to a despairing groan when a pupil gives a particularly inappropriate answer to a question. Several things however do bring a smile to the English teacher's face:

* *a good book*
* *excellent work*
* *school holidays*

Finally, though you can distinguish the English teacher by his solitary behaviour. On staff night's out, he has been known to engage in pack behaviour. But don't worry, he isn't dangerous!

Toolbox

A short natural history gives a brief summary of the essential facts about a wild animal:

* Habitat
* Appearance
* Behaviour

There is often a Latin name for the animal and a small map showing where in the world you will find it.

Use the present tense.

Use phrases to direct the reader:

* *It can be found in ...*
* *It likes ...*
* *It is a ... creature*
* *It is easy to spot*
* *It is distinguished by ...*
* *It has the following features*
* *Though it ..., it also ...*
* *It has even been known to ...*
* *Being a nocturnal creature, it tends to ...*

The writer can also use bullet points to put information across crisply.

Don't forget to sum up with a good last line.

Lesson 22

Newspaper reports

Lesson Plan

Objective: to write a newspaper report.

Stimulus: history topic books and a selection of newspaper reports.

Sentence level: variety of punctuation.

Shared writing: modelling of a first paragraph.

Guided writing: children write the story of the Battle of Hastings in the form of a newspaper report.

Structure of the lesson

Part 1

Ask the children to look at some newspaper headlines. How are they phrased? How many words do they use?

Now, how do the reports usually begin? What kind of phrases do they use? Make a list.

The teacher should then bring the pupils back together and discuss what they have noticed. She can then use this discussion to model the opening paragraph of a front page news report about the Battle of Hastings. Point out the way in which a newspaper, published to reach the doorstep the next morning, will look back at the day's events. It should make a generalised statement about the importance of the battle.

The children can then begin their own versions, armed with a good example.

Part 2

Describe the first engagements of the battle. Make it vivid. Include the sights and sounds of the skirmishes, picking out the main points. Remember to use some of the following in order to vary the text and keep the reader's attention:

- statements
- simple and complex sentences
- lists
- exclamations
- questions

Part 3

Describe the conclusion of the battle, including the death of King Harold. Use an eyewitness's quote. The closing sentences should also reflect on its outcome and draw out some lessons. The final sentence should tie things up, e.g. *Today's battle will go down in history.*

Examples of children's work

Daily Saxon
14th October, 1066
English suffer Hastings defeat!
King Harold slain in bloody encounter

By on-the-spot-reporter Sarah McHale, Year 5

Saxon England perished today in a bloody battle just outside Hastings. In the fighting King Harold was killed leaving the victorious William of Normandy to seize his crown.

Things began well for the English. Setting up his shield wall near the top of Caldbec Hill, King Harold adopted traditional Saxon tactics, first developed by Alfred the Great, daring William's troops to try to break his defensive line. With the advantage of the high ground, and using their shields well, the experienced House carls suffered few losses when the Normans fired their arrows. The Saxons, on the other hand, killed many Normans in a volley of missiles. There were even rumours that William had been killed. By midday, the tiring Normans seemed to be in real trouble.

It was at this point that William showed true leadership. Bravely, he lifted his helmet and urged his men forward. Cleverly pretending to retreat, the Normans tricked some of the Saxons, the less experienced fyrd men, down the hill and cut them to pieces. At last there was a break in the Saxon line. Firing over the heads of their own men, the Normans archers now caused havoc with their arrows. It was in one such hail of arrows that Harold was struck. Thrown into confusion by the death of their leader, the Saxons broke.

Eye witness Leofric of Somerset told the Daily Saxon: 'It was terrible. The dead and dying lay everywhere. I am broken-hearted.'

William had won a great victory. As I file this report, he is planning to march on London and claim the throne.

In summary, nothing will ever be the same after this decisive victory for the Normans. Could this even be the start of French rule? The Battle of Hastings will go down as a day when the history of England changed forever.

Comments

Sarah's report is coherent and well-organised. She uses newspaper-style conventions, such as the headline and sub-heading. She has a clear introduction summing up the significance of the event followed by a clear report of the main events. Finally, she summarises the lessons of the battle and concludes with a strong last line.

Suggestions

Other examples might be:
- the sinking of the Mary Rose
- Caesar's raid on Britain
- the Viking attack on Lindisfarne
- the burial of Tutenkhamun

Toolbox

Newspaper reports tell topical news stories directly and clearly.

Use a main headline and a supplementary headline.

Don't forget the date of the newspaper.

In the opening paragraph set out the main points of the report.

In the main part of the report, set out the main events in the past tense.

If appropriate, use quotations by some of the eye-witnesses or participants.

Consider these:
- lists
- statements

- simple and complex sentences
- questions
- exclamations

Conclude by summarising the main points or drawing out the reporter's conclusions or verdict on the events.

Lesson 23

Writing instructions: board games

Lesson Plan

Objective: to design a board game.

Stimulus: a selection of board games such as Monopoly. (This is the easiest format to reproduce with Year 5 or Year 6 children).

Sentence level: imperative sentences.

Shared writing: the teacher demonstrates the kind of instructions to put in each square (Go forward, Go back, Miss a go).

Guided writing: using a blank board game, the children write in their own instructions on the squares.

Structure of the lesson

Part 1

Give the children time to look at and discuss features of board games. Ask a secretary for each group to make notes. What text do they see? Discuss the conventions and how they work.

Part 2

Next, give the youngsters a template in the style of a Monopoly board. They should choose a number of squares (not too many, say eight altogether). Some will let the player go forward, some will tell them to go back. The children can then invent reasons for their forward or backward moves. The squares should include the instruction and the reason. These need to be short.

So, in a Boudicca Board Game, you might have:
• Ambush a Roman patrol – forward three spaces
• Capture a spy – forward two spaces
• Trinovantes squabbling – back four spaces
• Short of swords – back one space

Part 3

The children can then decorate the board and some of the squares. As an additional activity they could design chance cards featuring additional dangers and bonuses. These could be kept in a plastic wallet with the board game to which they belong.

Comments

This activity allows the children to explore instructional writing, using imperative sentences, while investigating design.

Some examples might be:
• a Star Wars board game
• the Viking board game
• the Battle of Hastings board game
• the Tutankhamun board game

Toolbox

Use a simple template with a numbered board.

There should be a bold title.

There should be good quality illustrations, a large one to draw attention to the game and smaller ones on some of the squares.

Use simple, imperative sentences:
• *Go forward*
• *Go back*
• *Miss a go*
• *Take an extra go*
• *Pick up a chance card*

Finally, as an extension, children can design their own chance cards.

Appendix 1

A note on note-taking

Note-taking is a supplementary activity to the main areas of non-fiction writing. It should be integrated into the main activities.

- Notes are short aids to jog your memory and remind you of facts and information you have learned in class.
- Notes should be as brief as possible – reduce them to keywords.
- Write down as many facts as you can remember for each keyword.
- You don't need to worry too much about punctuation.
- The notes should help you express things clearly and succinctly.
- Information sticks best if it is presented in different ways. Try diagrams, colour coding, flowcharts and other visual presentations.

One of the best ways to develop children's ability to incorporate note-taking in their repertoire is to make it a feature of the research section of some of the activities in this book, for example when gathering the information to write a biography.

The children could go on the Internet or browse information books in pairs. They would make brief notes summarising what they have learned for use in putting together their biography. During this part of the activity the teacher can intervene, showing what to include and what to leave out in order to make the note-taking efficient. Similarly, when doing the character sketches, the children could gather information about the character they are studying before starting work on the sustained composition.

All this works particularly well if incorporated into speaking and listening activities as a bridge to later writing.

Appendix 2

Bringing an author into school

Much of this book has been devoted to the notion of the teacher providing a model of the writing process, demonstrating to their students how to use language which is clear, expressive, imaginative, and even musical to communicate their ideas. There is, of course, another human resource which can be tapped and that is the writer.

Working with people who write for a living is a valuable experience. It demystifies writing and shows that it is something anyone can do. It demonstrates that expressing yourself through the medium of the written word can be both fun and emotionally rewarding. It helps introduce young people to the diversity and richness of contemporary British writing.

Writing Together is an initiative jointly organised by the Department for Education and Skills, QCA, Booktrust, Arts Council England and the Poetry Society. It is worth quoting at length from its publication *Bringing Writers into Schools*:

'Why a writer?

Inviting a writer into school:
- is inspiring and exciting for pupils and teachers
- encourages pupils to write and to see writing as worthwhile
- supports the teaching of both writing and reading
- pays dividends in pupils' development right across the curriculum, particularly in terms of planning, drafting and revising work
- encourages awareness of styles, imagery, structure and audience
- promotes the sharing of ideas and approaches
- helps young people to learn how inspiration is derived from a very wide range of sources
- provides a fresh awareness of the process and purpose of creative writing
- gives pupils the opportunity to think about how a book is created and where it all begins and ends
- promotes the idea of writing as a profession and writers as real people.'

Secretary of State for Education Charles Clarke says in the same booklet: 'Writing Together promotes creativity and raises standards because it brings together teachers, pupils and writers in a unique partnership. I am convinced of the value of writers in schools and look forward to these conferences developing effective approaches to writer visits and residencies so that they become a permanent part of the Key Stage 3 curriculum.'

For so many teachers who have often felt frustrated because of the pressures of a very prescriptive curriculum and testing regime, this can only come as a welcome statement. The only addendum I would make would be the Key Stage 1, 2 and 4 curriculums too.

Have clear objectives

It is important to have clear objectives. Do you want a long term or short term residence? What kind of writer do you want: a poet, a novelist, a non-fiction writer? With what age range will they be expected to work? Do you want them to give an author talk with questions and answers or would you like somebody who can lead writing workshops? Would the children benefit most from a mixture of the two? Will you incorporate sales of the author's books into the day? It should be self-evident that book ownership plays an extremely important part in encouraging young readers.

There are other considerations. What will be the outcome of the residence or visit? Will work be displayed around the school? Will it be published in an anthology or on the Internet? What follow-up will there be? Are parents or members of the local community going to be involved? Could you organise a celebration of achievement?

Find a suitable writer

Expect to pay a minimum fee of £250 a day, plus travel expenses and accommodation if required. Remember that writers have to earn a living too. For every J K Rowling, Jacqueline Wilson or Terry Pratchett there are hundreds of struggling writers. The Society of Authors estimates that 75% of authors receive an income comparable to a cleaner! This is a modest investment. Many schools invite several writers a year and their students gain a great deal from the experience. Information on funding can be found on the website of the National Literacy Trust: www.literacytrust.org.uk

Many authors have their own websites and you will be able to find out if they do school visits. You can also find writers who have experience of working in schools by contacting Booktrust, the Poetry Society, the National Association of Writers in Education or the various regional databases (information below). Your local library may also arrange visits by authors. Building a relationship with the library should be central to the ethos of the school anyway. The Artscape directory ensures that all individuals listed have enhanced disclosure checks from the Criminal Records Bureau and appropriate insurance.

Allow plenty of time between the initial contact and the visit. Many writers, especially those who have appeared on the shortlists of the many book awards, tend to be booked six to eight months ahead. I have lost count of the number of schools who have called me in February to ask if I can come on World Book Day in March. I usually answer: 'Which March?'

Practical advice

Agree the total cost, including travel and accommodation, well in advance. Check whether the author is VAT registered. If possible, arrange for the cheque to be ready on the day. If this is impractical, give the writer a rough idea when they can expect payment. The penniless writer waiting for a cheque to come in the post isn't completely fiction.

Have a clear line of communication: a phone number or email address. Arrange for the author to be picked up if they are coming by public transport. If they are driving, make sure they have a map and clear directions well in advance.

Negotiate the timetable of events with the writer. Don't spring a list of demands on them on arrival. This will only cause tension. Discuss the room in which they will work and check what equipment they will need. Do your best to avoid interruptions. Dragging children out of an engrossing session to see the dentist or attend an assembly is hugely frustrating and counter-productive.

Make arrangements for breaks and for lunch. The author should be provided with a bottle of spring water during sessions. Coffee and biscuits during breaks always go down well. Lunch should be provided. Check dietary requirements in advance. Don't expect the writer to fend for him or herself. Remember, they are in unfamiliar surroundings. We all need a little TLC. I heard of one famous poet who asked for a school lunch. He was told no and had to eat fish and chips on the sea front!

Prepare the children in advance. They should be familiar with at least one of the writer's titles. It helps to have looked up the author's website. Do your homework. I was once introduced to 200 Year 8s as follows:

'This is...what was your name again? ... Right, this is Mr Gibson ... What ... Oh, Gibbons! I'm afraid I haven't read any of your books, but teachers are busy people. Well, this is Year 8. Off you go.'

Make sure the writer is supported at all times. Don't leave them alone with 32 children. Don't do your marking at the back. Get involved. Working with a writer acts as INSET. What's more, it is enjoyable and enriching.

Contact the local media to publicise the visit. It is good for the school, good for the writer and good for the pupils.

Useful contacts

The Arts Councils give practical advice on organising school visits and are involved in other arts and literature initiatives . Academi gives part funding to school visits in Wales. Booktrust is a charity which promotes reading. It has been involved in the *Writing Together* initiative linking writers and schools, and organises the Booktrust Teenage Prize. NAWE publishes a magazine about writers who work in education and is involved in coordinating the work of creative writers in education. The Poetry Society runs activities introducing poets to schools. Apples and Snakes and The Windows Project both have a register of writers who will visit schools. The Arvon Foundation organises long-term residential courses at its centres around the country. The other organisations also do similar work promoting writers in schools.

Arts Council England
Tel: 0845 300 6200

Scottish Arts Council
Tel: 0131 226 6051
www.scottisharts.org.uk

Arts Council of Wales
Tel: 02920 376500
www.artswales.org

Arts Council of Northern Ireland
Tel: 028 9038 5200
www.artscouncil-ni.org

Academi
www.academi.org

Booktrust
Tel: 020 8516 2977
info@booktrust.org.uk
www.booktrusted.com

The National Association of Writers in Education (NAWE)
Tel: 01653 618429
info@nawe.co.uk

The Poetry Society
Tel: 020 7420 9894
education@poetrysociety.org.uk
www.poetrysociety.org.uk

Apples and Snakes
Tel: 020 7738 0941
jasper@applesandsnakes.org
www.applesandsnakes.org

The Arvon Foundation
Tel: 020 7931 7611
b.lyon@arvonfoundation.org
www.arvonfoundation.org

Book Communications
Tel: 0121 246 2777
jonathan@bookcommunications.co.uk

PEN – Readers and Writers
Tel: 020 7713 0023
wwwenglishpen.org/readersandwriters

Royal Festival Hall Literature Education
Tel: 020 7921 0867
sasha@rfh.org.uk

The Windows Project
Tel: 0151 709 3688
windows@windowsproject.demon.co.uk
www.windowsproject.demon.co.uk

New Writing North
Tel: 0191 232 9991
mail@newwritingnorth.com
www.newwritingnorth.com

Poetry Can
Tel: 0117 942 6976
info@poetrycan.demon.co.uk